MARK: REALISTIC THEOLOGIAN

In memory of
Damian Byrne
Dominican

Wilfrid J. Harrington, O.P.

Mark: Realistic Theologian
The Jesus of Mark

the columba press

First published, 1996, by
the columba press
55A Spruce Avenue, Stillorgan Industrial Park,
Blackrock, Co Dublin

This new revised edition, 2002

Cover by Bill Bolger
The image from the Book of Kells is used by permission of
The Board of Trinity College Dublin.
Origination by The Columba Press
Printed in Ireland by Colour Books Ltd, Dublin

ISBN 1 85607 390 4

Acknowledgement
I thank my friends Michael Glazier and Seán O Boyle. They have
read my manuscript. Their encouragement is comfort. Their practical
suggestions make for a better text.

Contents

Preface   7

Introduction   8

Chapter One   Mark   11

Chapter Two   Jesus   21

Chapter Three   Prophet   31

Chapter Four   Teacher   49

Chapter Five   Healer   74

Chapter Six   Exorcist   86

Chapter Seven   Messiah   97

Chapter Eight   The Cross   124

Conclusion   141

Notes   145

For Reference and Further Study   148

Index of Marcan Passages   150

Preface

The gospel of Mark is a taut text. Behind the text is a brilliant story-teller and a thoughtful theologian. Increasingly, Mark has become my favourite gospel. I believe I admire most his realism. My own more recent work on the book of Revelation (with its focus on the slain Lamb) confirms my conviction that the cross is indeed the heart of Christianity – the heart as understood by Paul and Mark and the author of Revelation.[1] Mark's gospel is a theology of the cross. Before the cross there is no place to hide. All human life is there.

I attempt to present the Jesus of Mark's faith. A presumptuous endeavour, I acknowledge. I myself am so convinced that Mark had got it right that I take the risk of being presumptuous. I would wish my readers to go to Mark. All I can expect is that I may have alerted them to aspects of the gospel that, perhaps, they may not have hitherto observed. Mark will do the rest. Mark remains, as he well knows, a pointer. It is the Jesus of Mark who matters. I find that the Jesus of Mark is the Lord of my Christian faith. Perhaps those who think so may be helped by this presentation. Others may be nudged to think again. For all of us the question stands: "Who, then, is this?"

Introduction

Mark, it can be argued, had pioneered the gospel form, had invented the literary form "gospel." He had wanted to present the kerygma, the proclamation of the Good News, and had hit on the design of setting it in the framework of a schematized life of Jesus. Mark was keenly aware that the revelation of salvation takes place in the real world of human existence. It was, then, altogether fitting that God's saving purpose should be in terms of the human life of Jesus Christ. Inspired by this insight the gospel is subtle and complex. It could not be otherwise as the author seeks to express, in terms of a human life, the startling fact of divine presence in our world, with the tensions that truth involves.

For Mark, God was surely present in Jesus of Nazareth. His Jesus was the *man* who, at Gethsemane, besought his God to pass from him the cup of suffering, who experienced on that cross of suffering the awfulness of God-forsakenness. Mark's christology was not Chalcedonian – it could not have been. His christology is thoroughly Christian and profoundly challenging. Marcan christology is not inferior to other New Testament christologies. It is different. Christianity is about reality. Mark was a realistic theologian. In authentically Christian fashion his realism is manifest in his christology – in his portrait of Jesus Christ.

Mark is clear, and uncompromisingly uncomfortable, in his christological position and in his understanding of discipleship. His perspective is certainly clear in one predominant aspect: suffering Messiahship and suffering discipleship. Mark's Christian faith is firmly anchored in the risen Lord. But he is keenly conscious of living "between the times": between the resurrection and the consummation. Victory is the destiny of the faithful Christian. But life in the here and now is real and earnest and can be grim. Mark acknowledges that Christian existence is paradoxical. He finds it normal that it should be so. Jesus won his victory through suffering and death. There is, for him, no other way of Christian living nor path to Christian victory. Mark has written that his Christians should understand and accept this. Mark is a realistic theologian. His realism finds expression, primarily, in his christology.

For us, Christians, God is not an abstraction nor authentic humanness only an ideal. True, whole humanness has been lived among us. Jesus of Nazareth, "the reflection of God's glory and the exact imprint of God's very being," is one who had become "like his brothers and sisters in every respect" (Heb 1:3; 2:17). Up to the launching of his brief ministry he had lived an uneventful life. During that public phase he was to rouse more opposition than support. He was not immune to suffering, not even from the agony of an atrocious and humiliating death. The fact that he was "without sin" (4:15) did not imply any lack of humanness. Sin – though we all are sinners – is *not* an intrinsic ingredient of humanness. It is a fall from humanness.

In maintaining that Jesus of Nazareth was wholly human, I am not suggesting that he was "merely" human. He is the one in whom God is wholly present, the one through whose life and deeds and words God has spoken his final word to humankind.[2] For me, the absolute conviction that in the man Jesus of Nazareth my God is wholly present is basis of my faith and life. It is so beyond any theological speculation. As the human person in whom God is fully present, Jesus has defined God for us. All authentic religion is, in some measure, revelation of God. What is distinctive of Christian religion is that *Jesus* is revelation of God. He tells us who God is and what God is like: he is the God "made flesh" in Jesus. Traditionally, our theology has put the cart before the horse by striving to explain Jesus in terms of God. It is by accepting, totally, the humanness of Jesus of Nazareth that we, to the limit of our human intelligence, can attain knowledge of God. And it is by perception of the humanness of Jesus that we gain a right understanding of humanness.

Jesus is the Messiah, of that Mark is sure – but he is a disconcerting Messiah. The question stands, writ large: Who, then, is this? That Jesus would have permitted himself to be taken by his enemies, to be maltreated and mocked by them, and put to death, is something that the contemporaries of Jesus and the readers of Mark could scarcely comprehend. Yet, if one has not come to terms with this "scandal" one has not grasped the originality of Jesus, in particular, the Jesus portrayed by Mark. Jesus did not come as judge with sentence and punishment for those who will not receive the gift of forgiveness and salvation he offered them. He has come as the one who will let himself be crushed by the evil intent of those who resist him and would be rid of him.

In the long run, what is incomprehensible is the rejection and violent death of the promised Messiah who would reveal the Father. The originality of Jesus flows from the contrast between his heavenly authority and power and the humiliation of his crucifixion. Mark's "messianic secret" is designed to reconcile two theological affirmations: Jesus, from the first, was indeed Messiah; yet, he had to receive from the Father, through the abasement of the cross, his title of Messiah. The meaning of his life is that as Son of God sent by the Father, he had come to deliver humans from all their enemies. He came to forgive sins, not to chastise sinners. He came, but he will not impose. When it came to the test, rather than force the human heart, he humbled himself and permitted himself to be taken and shamed and put to death.

Jesus of Nazareth was a complex character. He was a man of his time: a first-century Galilean Jew. In the context of his religious tradition he was in the line of the prophets and sages of Israel. He was healer and exorcist. By some he, likely, was perceived as a messianic figure. Mark accepted all that. For him, there was a further and decisive dimension. He viewed Jesus and his message in the light of his resurrection faith. His Jesus was Messiah and Son of God. He does not use the confessional formula of early Christians: *Kyrios Iésous Christos* (Jesus Christ is Lord) – but, in practice, he subscribed to it. All he has written of Jesus is shot-through with his Christian faith. This should be kept in mind throughout our presentation. Still, Mark, better than the other evangelists, helps us to glimpse that man of Nazareth who, for a few short years, in the little land of Palestine, bore unparalleled witness to the God of Israel and of humankind.

CHAPTER 1

Mark

*I decided to know nothing among you except Jesus Christ,
and him crucified.* (1 Cor 2:2).

Underestimated from early times because of its brevity (almost all
of Mark is found in Matthew and Luke) in our day the gospel of
Mark has come into its own. Above all, the evangelist Mark stands
side by side with Paul as a stalwart proclaimer of a *theologia crucis* –
a theology of the cross. And, congenial to modern christology, the
Marcan Jesus is the most human in the gospels. Mark sets the pattern of a gospel: it is concerned with christology and discipleship.
Jesus is Son of God, that is, God-appointed leader of the new
covenant people; he is "son of man", the human one who came to
serve, the one faithful unto death. One who has come to terms with
the cross (with the meaning of his death) can know him and can
confess him – like the centurion (Mark 15:39). His disciples did not
understand him before Calvary. The Christian reader of the first
century, and of today, is being challenged to come to terms with the
love of God shown forth in the cross of Jesus.

STORY

The setting
The view that Mark had written in Rome about 65 A.D. and for people
in Rome, has long been the prevalent one. But it has not gone
unchallenged because the traditional data which point to this
provenance and date are of uncertain worth. We are forced back to
the text of the gospel: to an anonymous writing of the first Christian
century. The author is not named in the gospel; the traditional
name Mark was quite common. Nothing in the gospel points necessarily to a Roman origin. We can be sure that "Mark" wrote for a
specific community and in face of the actual circumstances of that
community. We are left to tease out a plausible setting for, and a
likely date of, his gospel.

Today we confidently set the writing of the gospel close to the events of the Jewish war of 66-70 A.D. A careful reading of Mark 13 would suggest a date soon after the Roman destruction of Jerusalem in 70 A.D. With mounting scholarly opinion I would propose that Mark was written to and for a Christian community somewhere in the Roman province of Syria. This would offer a setting close to the tragic events of the war. The community may even have harboured Christian refugees from the conflict, making it that much more immediate.

The gospel of Mark, after an introduction (1:1-13) which sets the stage for the drama that follows, is built up of two complementary parts. The first (1:14-8:30) is concerned with the mystery of Jesus' identity; it is dominated by the question, "Who is Jesus?" The emphasis in this part of Mark is on Jesus' miracles; the teaching is largely parabolic. The second part (8:31-16:8) is concerned with the messianic destiny of Jesus: a way of suffering and death. The emphasis in this second half of Mark is on Jesus' teaching which, now directed at his disciples, builds upon their recognition of him as Messiah and is concerned mainly with the nature of his messiahship and with the suffering it will entail both for himself and for his followers.

Plot and characters

A gospel, addressed to a Christian community, has the concerns and needs of the community in mind. These are concerns and needs perceived by the evangelist (not necessarily by the recipients, or not, at least, by all of them). His readers know the basic story as well as the author. He makes his point by telling the story in his way. It is story: with plot and characters. Each of the evangelists tells essentially the same story (manifestly true of the synoptists), but the plots and emphases of the gospels differ considerably. The events and actions of a story, its plot, regularly involve conflict; indeed, conflict (not necessarily violent conflict) is the heart of most stories. Not alone do the gospels have plots but the plot is, in a sense, an evangelist's interpretation of the story. As writers of narrative literature, the evangelists achieved their purpose by means of plot and characterisation.

Characterisation refers to the manner in which a narrative brings characters to life in a story. In literary terms, "characters" are not the same as people. In day-to-day life we know one another imperfectly. I may guess at your thoughts; I cannot really know what you are thinking. Characters can be transparent. The narrator may fully expose a character to one's readers, can permit the reader to get inside the character. Alternatively, one can present a "true" picture of any character. The gospels, in which Jesus is a literary character, make him known to us more profoundly than he, as a person, was in fact known to his contemporaries.

The distinction between "character" and "person" is very important. Jesus of Nazareth was a wholly historical person. He was a first-century Palestinian Jew who carried out what – he was convinced – was a God-given mission to his people. He was rejected, and was condemned and executed by an alliance of Jewish religious and Roman political authorities. The "character" Jesus of the gospels is this Jesus now viewed through Christian eyes, seen through the prism of resurrection-faith. Each gospel has several characters, of varying importance for the flow of the story. Jesus is always the chief character; the evangelist speaks, primarily, through him. Jesus carries the central message of each gospel. And Jesus is chief spokesman of an evangelist's concern.

THE PLOT

As in most stories, the events and action of the Marcan story involve conflict, and Jesus is the immediate cause of the conflict. We may illustrate by glancing, firstly, at conflicts between Jesus and the authorities, and then at those between Jesus and his disciples.

Jesus versus the authorities

The authorities involved were the religious and political leaders – and in relation to them Jesus was at a disadvantage. Mark does indeed show Jesus having facile authority over evil spirits – the exorcisms, and over nature – the stilling of the storm. But Jesus' authority did not extend to lording it over people. Still, what Jesus said and did challenged directly the authorities of Israel. For their part, the authorities viewed themselves as defenders of God's Law. They contended that Jesus assumed unwarranted legal authority for himself, interpreted the law in a manner they considered illegal,

and disregarded many religious customs. They responded by uttering charges against him.

Jesus, for his part, had been anointed to usher in God's rule (1:9-11).
The issue for him was how to get the authorities to "see" God's
authority in his actions and teaching. The narrator skillfully created
tension and suspense. By the end of the five conflict-stories (2:1-3:6)
the sides are clearly established (3:6). The impending clash with the
authorities is kept in sight during the journey to Jerusalem (8:27-
10:52). The climactic confrontation in Jerusalem came quickly. It is
noteworthy that the first accusation against Jesus was a charge of
blasphemy: "Why does this man speak in this way? It is blasphemy!"
(2:7) – thus, from the start of the story Jesus walks a tightrope.
Nevertheless, the reader recognises that Jesus is firmly in control.
At the trial he himself volunteered the evidence his accusers needed.
"'Are you the Messiah, the son of the Blessed one?' Jesus answered
'I am'" (14:61-62). Jesus, not the authorities, determined his fate.

The narrator resolves the conflict between the authorities only
when they condemned Jesus and put him to death. It was an ironic
resolution. The authorities had, unwittingly, co-operated in bringing to pass God's purpose. By means of this ironic resolution the
story depicts Jesus as the real authority in Israel. The authorities
condemned as blasphemy Jesus' claim to be Son of God but, since in
the story world Jesus' claim is true, they are the ones guilty of blasphemy. The irony is hidden from the authorities, but it is not hidden from the reader. The reader knows that Jesus will be established in
power and the authorities condemned (8:28-9:1; 13:24-27, 30-32;
14:62).

Jesus and the disciples

At stake in the conflict with the disciples is whether Jesus can make
them good disciples. The disciples struggled at every point to follow Jesus but were simply overwhelmed both by him and by his
demands. Jesus' efforts to lead the disciples to understand were
matched by their fear and their hardness of heart. Theirs was not
the determined opposition to Jesus of the authorities – they were
trying to be his followers. They did consistently misunderstand
Jesus' teaching and ended up by failing him utterly. Yet, they had
followed him to Jerusalem. Jesus just could not lead his chosen dis-

ciples (effectively, the Twelve) to understand him, could not get
them to do what he expected of them. In an effort to bring them to
realize how dense and blind they were, he hurled challenging questions at them (4:13,40; 8:17-21,33; 9:19; 14:37,41) – and was met with
silence. He tried to prepare them for his impending death and for
his absence. He knew that they would fail him in Jerusalem; yet he
sought to urge them to stand by him (14:37, 41-42). The outer conflict reflects an inner conflict within the disciples: they want to be
loyal to Jesus, but not at the cost of giving up everything, least of all
their lives. The fact remains that readers of the gospel are most likely
to empathise with those same disciples. By doing so the readers
come to discern their own inadequacies. They find comfort in the
realisation that, although the disciples failed him, Jesus remained
unflinchingly faithful to them.

Jesus did not, however, manage to make them faithful disciples.
They failed him – and the question stands: will they learn from their
failure and, beyond his death, at last become truly followers of him?
When Jesus had warned his followers of their impending failure
(14:26-31) he had added a reassuring word: "After I am raised up, I
will go before you to Galilee" (14:28). That word is then caught up
in the message of the "young man" at the tomb: "Go, tell his disciples and Peter that he is going before you to Galilee; there you will
see him, just as he told you" (16:7). Throughout the gospel "to see"
Jesus means to have faith in him. What Mark is saying is that if the
community is to "see" Jesus, now the Risen One, it must become
involved in the mission to the world that "Galilee" signified.
Galilee was the place of mission, the arena where Jesus' exorcisms
and healings had broken the bonds of evil. There, too, the disciples
had been called and commissioned to take up Jesus' proclamation
of the coming rule of God. "Galilee" is the place of the universal
mission. But no disciple is ready to proclaim the gospel until she or
he has walked the way to Jerusalem (10:32-34) and encountered the
reality of the cross.

THE CHARACTERS

Characters are a central element of the story world. The narrator
brings characters to life either as one "tells" the reader directly what
characters are like or as one "shows" the characters by having them
speak and act, or by having others talk about them and speak to them.

Jesus

The narrator of Mark tends to show the characters to the reader. Obviously, Jesus is the dominant character and his characterization is, not surprisingly, complex. Jesus speaks and acts: what he says discloses his understanding of himself and of his mission; what he does reveals the extent of his authority from God. In Mark's story, Jesus was proclaimed God's Son at his baptism, for it was then that God declared Jesus to be Son and anointed him with the Holy Spirit (1:9-11). This was a decisive experience for Jesus. Henceforth, he was convinced that through him "the rule of God has come near" (1:15). But, if Jesus did have *exousia* – authority – from God, that power of his did not have any shade of domination. The hallmark of the use of his authority in relation to people (as distinct from his authority over evil and nature) was consistently, and emphatically, that of *diakonia* (service).

The death of Jesus was wholly consonant with his understanding of authority. He was the one who had come to serve. And if he spoke of renouncing self, being least and losing one's life (8:34-37), his living of all this lent unanswerable authority to his word. Mark sees clearly (as Paul, before him, had grasped) that the death of Jesus set the seal of authenticity on every single word and deed of him. Mark makes his point superbly by presenting the death of Jesus as a disaster, without any relieving feature at all. Mark does not veil the awesome nature of death. Death is abandonment, isolation, and separation. Paradoxically, the *theologia crucis* of Paul and Mark is a surer ground of hope than a *theologia gloriae* which has little to answer to the harsh question of reality.

The minor characters

The narrator shows the authorities in a consistently negative light. The disciples – in practice, the Twelve – are presented in an unflattering light. In contrast, the characterisation of the minor characters is firmly positive. Here, indeed, is an eye-opener. One's attention is drawn to something so obvious that it had escaped our attention. The fact is that, over against both opponents and disciples, minor characters in the gospel steadfastly exemplify the values of the rule of God. Mark seems to be reminding his community that the sterling Christian qualities are to be found in the "simple faithful."

The narrator developed these "little people" as foils to the authorities and disciples, and as parallels to Jesus. These minor characters do measure up to Jesus' standards – especially as they exemplify the values of faith, of being least, of willingness to serve. In the first half of the gospel they measure up to Jesus' opening summons: "be converted, and believe in the good news" (for example, 1:29-31,40-45; 5:18-20, 21-43; 7:24-30, 31-37; 8:22-27). In the final scenes, in Jerusalem, the minor characters exemplify especially the teaching about being "servant of all." Where, before, Jesus had served others now, in his time of need, others served him. The consistent conduct of the "little people" stands in sharp contrast to the conduct of the Twelve. In the first half of the story, while there is no direct comparison, the minor characters emerge as models of faith – more than could be said of the Twelve. In the last scenes in Jerusalem the minor characters do fulfill the functions expected of disciples. Here the "little people" are highlighted (10:46-52; 14:3-9; 15:40-41; 16:1-8). Henceforth, any enlightened reading of Mark's gospel must acknowledge the major contribution of its minor characters.[3]

Narrative criticism

Since Mark is indeed a literary work, application of the method of narrative criticism has provided valuable insights. In narrative criticism "meaning" is found in the encounter between the text and the reader. While narrative critics do not repudiate the finding of historical-critical scholarship (for that matter, historical criticism and narrative criticism are complementary) they do ask different questions of the text. If the answer is, in each case, different, it is because the question is other. We may here instance a passage where the answer to the narrative critical question throws fresh light on a celebrated problem in Mark.

The Ending (16:8). In 16:1-8 Mark relates that the three women named in 15:40, intending to anoint the body of Jesus, came to the tomb when the sabbath had ended. There a "young man" (an angel) informed them that the crucified Jesus of Nazareth whom they sought was "not here": he had been raised. The women were given a message for the Twelve: Jesus is going before them into Galilee (16:7). But, what kind of messengers did they turn out to be? For, disconcertingly, the closing statement runs: "So they went out and fled from the tomb, for terror and amazement had seized them; and they said nothing to anyone, for they were afraid" (16:8).

The abrupt ending of Mark has long been seen as a problem. Early Christians had been puzzled by this startling closure of the gospel. Attempts were made to round off Mark's work. The manuscript tradition has preserved three different endings – notably the familiar *Longer Ending* (16:9-20). Narrative critics rightly view 16:8 not only as Mark's intended ending but as a classic example of the literary feature of unresolved conflict. Its purpose is to involve the readers. They are made to wonder how they would have acted had they found themselves in the situation of these women. The open-ended Marcan conclusion challenges and demands response. The Marcan story is not rounded-off precisely because the readers are asked to write its ending. "It remains to be seen whether we, confident of the victory of the Lord of life, will quietly and passionately minister in his name in our Galilee – the boardroom, factories, homes, relationships, voting booths, pulpits – to which Christ sends us. Yet one thing is sure: He has gone there ahead of us, and there we can see him, just as he promised."[4]

Reader response criticism

How do we as readers respond to Mark's gospel? This question brings up what has become known as reader response criticism. The focus here is not on evangelist or text but on the reader and her or his responses to the text. Our response is inevitably influenced by our own presuppositions and prejudices. These, in fact, play a larger role in interpretation than we imagine. And, of course, our modern responses are not necessarily the same as those of the first readers/hearers of the gospel. In short, for a balanced interpretation we should keep in mind that the evangelist, his text, and the reader all have their place.

THE GOSPEL AND THE MAN

"Who then is this?" (4:41). The question was wrung from the awestruck disciples of Jesus when, at his word, a great calm had fallen upon the troubled waters and their storm-tossed boat had come to rest. For Mark, that chastened crew might have been the community, the little church for whom he wrote. He wrote for people such as they who needed to know Jesus, who wanted to understand who he really was. He wrote for Christians who doubted and were fearful: "Teacher, do you not care if we perish?" (v 38). He wrote for Christians who did not relish the idea of being disciples of a suffering Messiah. He wrote for Christians very like ourselves. His gospel is a tract for our time.

We may ask, what of Mark? His gospel shows him to be a writer of great natural talent, a man with an eye for a telling detail, a man who could effectively structure his material. Mark emerges, too, as a theologian of stature. Some have argued for a Pauline influence on Mark. Whatever of that, the Christ of Mark is a Christ whom Paul could recognize and the gospel of Mark is one which Paul would not have disdained to call his own. Mark's gospel is the gospel of Jesus Christ, the "Son of God" and closes with the resounding declaration: "Truly, this man was God's Son!" And yet, his Jesus is a man who was indignant and angry, who took children into his arms, a man who suffered and died. This Son of Man who came "not to be served but to serve, and to give his life as a ransom for many" (10:45) is the Christ whom Paul preached: "When I came to you, brothers and sisters, I did not come proclaiming the mystery of God to you in lofty words or wisdom. For I decided to know nothing among you except Jesus Christ, and him crucified" (1 Cor 2:1-2). Paul the apostle, the first great Christian theologian, had come to terms with the scandal of the cross. Mark the evangelist is, perhaps, the next notable Christian theologian in line.

Mark's spirituality

In current usage, spirituality is a broad and elusive term. Christian spirituality is, perhaps, best understaood as *faith*, lived in *love*, sustained by *hope*. Our faith is trust in God, whose graciousness has been fully revealed in and through Jesus Christ. Christian life is faith-inspired life. It is a way marked by *love* – love of God and of one another. It is a *koinónia* – fellowship. Our Christian life is pilgrimage; we need to be sure that we do not journey toward a mirage. Our *hope*, like our faith, is based on the faithfulness of our God, the God we meet in the Son. Because of the suffering and death of the Son, our star of hope shines for us beyond suffering, beyond death itself.

Mark's gospel is a model of Christian spirituality. Jesus displays trust in his Father and insistently calls for faith. He shows love for all, especially the marginalised, and demands that we serve one another in love. Mark's theology of the cross is, paradoxically, the surest ground of hope. The response to Jesus' cry of Godforsakenness was his vindication through resurrection. As for positive response to Jesus within the gospel, that came exclusively from 'marginal' figures – notably women. This should not surprise us. After all, Jesus had declared: 'it is to such as these that the kingdom of God belongs' (10:14). Our response to Mark's spirituality demands humility. 'Let anyone with ears to hear listen!' (4:9)

CHAPTER 2

Jesus

For we do not have a high priest who is unable to sympathize with our weaknesses, but we have one who in every respect has been tested as we are, yet without sin ... Therefore he had to become like his brothers and sisters in every respect. (Heb 4:15; 1:17).

"We believe in one Lord, Jesus Christ, the only Son of God ..." There is a wealth of christology behind this credal statement, this proclamation of Christian faith. It is helpful – needful indeed – to map the areas of faith and history. We find Jesus in both, as the "real" Jesus and as a scholarly construct. We learn from both perspectives. And what we discern aids us in our appreciation of the Jesus of the gospels. Here, in modest compass, we look to the "historical" Jesus.

I. THE REAL JESUS

The object of Christian faith is the person Jesus Christ who once lived, briefly, on earth in the first century A.D. and now lives on in the Father's presence. The subject matter of the gospels is this Jesus Christ. The gospels, at once historical and theological, proclaim Jesus of Nazareth as the Christ, the definitive revelation of God. The proclaimed Jesus is a construct of Christian theological and spiritual imagination aimed at eliciting a faith response. The proclamation embraces strictly historical elements (e.g. Jesus' death on the cross) and theological interpretation in terms of biblical categories (e.g. ascent to God's right hand).

What [the gospels] give us is the Jesus-image, or the proclaimed Jesus who actually lived and died in first-century Palestine, who now reigns gloriously as Savior of the world, who indwells his followers of this and every age and who is the Christ in whom God is definitively and salvifically revealed ... The real Jesus is precisely the proclaimed Jesus. Part of the Jesus-image, and a

21

constitutive and irreducible part, is the actual earthly career of Jesus of Nazareth that is the heart of the image. [5]

The real or actual Jesus is the glorified Saviour alive in our midst. He will always be shrouded in mystery. The total reality of any person is unknowable to human discernment – how much more the reality of the Risen One. The gospels present us with "the earthly Jesus": a picture of Jesus during his life on earth. Their partial, and theologically coloured, pictures serve as the source for the theoretical construct "the historical Jesus." The historical Jesus is not the real Jesus, but only a fragmentary hypothetical reconstruction of him by modern means of research.

Theology, the study of faith, if it is to be credible and effective, must reflect the culture within which it takes shape. Modern christology, then, has to take cognisance of historical-critical concern and has to accommodate the quest for the historical Jesus. After all, if faith is adherence to a particular person, we will want to know all we can about this person. Besides, there has been a deep-rooted tendency, in the name of "orthodoxy", to stress so the divinity of Jesus that his humanity has almost been lost to sight. Emphasis on the historical Jesus reminds us that the risen Christ is the same person who lived and suffered and died in first-century Palestine, a man as wholly human as any human person. Again, in Christian history and practice, Jesus has been effectively domesticated. Historical research has brought to light a challenging and embarrassing nonconformist Jesus.

The historical Jesus is not coextensive with the Jesus of the gospel narratives. There is much in the gospel narratives that is not historical. The gospel picture is "accurate" not in the sense that it is exact in detail but that it is truth-bearing. It is the acceptance of it by the early believing community that guarantees the substantial truth of the gospel account. The gospel Jesus is more than the historical Jesus: the gospel presents not only history but the transhistorical, not only fact but theological interpretation. On the other hand, the ecclesiastical proclamation of the Jesus-image is often less than, is unfaithful to, the historical Jesus in which the image is rooted. This is a further reason for investigation of and discernment of the historical Jesus.

II. THE HISTORICAL JESUS

Jesus of Nazareth was a first-century A.D. Jew who began, lived, and ended his short life in Palestine, a minor province of the Roman Empire. Our information about him, by historical standards, is meagre. Apart from two brief statements, by the Jewish historian Flavius Josephus and the Roman historian Tacitus respectively, our sources for knowledge of the historical Jesus are the canonical gospels alone. A summary of the historical facts about Jesus of Nazareth, based on the meticulous research of a major New Testament scholar, will serve our purpose. [6]

Around 7-4 B.C., that is, toward the close of the reign of Herod the Great, a Jewish boy, to be named Jesus (Yeshua), was born, either in Bethlehem of Judea or Nazareth of Galilee. His mother was named Mary (Miryam), his putative father Joseph (Yosef). He grew up in Nazareth and was known as "the Nazarene". His native language was Aramaic; he would have had a practical command of Greek. It is highly likely that he was literate; as a boy he would have been taught in the village synagogue. Like Joseph (Mt 13:55) Jesus (Mk 6:3) was a *tektón* – most probably a carpenter. In a small village, Joseph's would have been the only carpenter shop; the family would have had a frugally comfortable life-style.

The gospels speak of the "brothers (and sisters)" of Jesus. The most striking passage is Mark 6:3 – "Is not this the carpenter, the son of Mary and brother of James and Judas and Simon, and are not his sisters here with us?" Throughout the New Testament the word *adelphos* ("brother"), when not used metaphorically, means a blood brother – whether full or half brother. It is most natural, then, to regard these brothers and sisters of Jesus as his siblings. It is, nonetheless, not unreasonable, on theological grounds, to take the term in a broader sense. At the same time, it should be noted that the tradition of the virginal conception of Jesus (which, strictly speaking, would not necessarily exclude his having brothers and sisters) is found only in the Infancy Narratives (Mt 1-2; Lk 12-2) – and these are profoundly christological texts. The point is: a definite answer to these questions is beyond the scope of historical-critical research. But the questions are there.

Not controversial is the fact that Jesus of Nazareth was a layman,

who lived in the quiet obscurity of a Galilean village. It is not surprising that the gospels (outside the Passion Narratives) show no
evidence of any dialogue with the Jerusalem priests. They would
have had no interest in a Galilean layman – until they began to perceive him as a threat. The letter to the Hebrews does, of course,
elaborate a theology of the priesthood of Christ. It is precisely that:
a theological construct – the heavenly priesthood of the Risen One.
The author is perfectly aware that the earthly Jesus was not a priest:

> Now if he were on earth, he would not be a priest at all, since
> there are priests who offer gifts according to the law (8:4).

> It is evident that our Lord was descended from Judah, and in con-
> nection with that tribe Moses said nothing about priests (7:14).

In our western world we have a fascination with dates and times –
birthdays, and so on. When one really thinks about it, such precis-
ion is not of much importance. I was born, I will die – this is the reality that is mightily important to me; marks on a calendar are of little
significance. It matters little that we are unable to date precisely the
birth, ministry and death of Jesus. We may, at best, propose a fair
approximation:

Birth	7-6 B.C.
Beginning of Ministry	A.D. 28. If Jesus began his ministry early in 28, it would have lasted a little over two years.
Death	A.D. 30. 14 Nisan – eve of Passover. Jesus would have been about thirty-six at his death.

We turn to some aspects of Jesus' ministry and death.

III. DISCIPLE OF THE BAPTIST

In all four gospels, before the ministry of Jesus opens, John the
Baptist is introduced. According to the synoptic gospels (not, however, in the fourth gospel) Jesus was baptized by John. Who is this
John? In his *Jewish Antiquities* the Jewish historian Flavius Josephus
writes of the execution of John by Herod Antipas. He has it in the
context of his account of the defeat of Herod by the Nabatean King

Aretas IV in 36 A.D. In his judgment the defeat was retribution for Herod's slaying of John. He describes John, surnamed the Baptist, as one who baptized Jews who "were cultivating virtue and practising justice toward one another and piety toward God." Because John had won a notable following, Herod feared that his popularity might spark a revolt. He decided on a pre-emtive strike and had John arrested and sent in chains to Machaerus, a fortress south of the Dead Sea. There John was put to death. This account of the death of the Baptist is preferable to the evidently legendary story of Mark 6:17-29.

John the Baptist

It is clear from Josephus' text (and he has more to say of the Baptist than of Jesus) that John had been a prominent figure. This is borne out by the gospels. Paradoxically, they witness to the importance of the Baptist by consistently cutting him down to size. In Mark (1:2-11) the Baptizer is he who would prepare the way for "one who is more powerful than I". He was unaware that Jesus was the mightier one. In Matthew (3:13-15) John recognized Jesus' status and acknowledged his own inferiority. In Luke (1:41-44; 3:19-21) Jesus, cousin of John, met with John; it is not explicitly stated that he was baptized by John; the implication is there. In the fourth gospel John is not given the title Baptist – there is an oblique reference to his practice of baptizing (1:25-26). There is no place for the baptism of Jesus by John. Here the *raison d'être* of John is to witness to Jesus (1:7-8, 19, 23, 29, 34; 3:29-30).

It is evident that early Christians were increasingly uneasy at this baptism of their Jesus by the Baptist – embarrassment is evident in Mt 3:13-14. The reaction underlines the firm historicity of the occurrence: they were stuck with the fact. The matter is complicated by the characterisation of John's baptism as "a baptism of repentance for the forgiveness of sins" (Mk 1:4). This made Jesus' submission to John's baptism even more problematic. In John's estimation, however, his baptism was not only a sign of the candidates' repentance but pledge of new life, of a radical change. It was too, symbolically, an anticipation of an ultimate total cleansing of sin. In this perspective, a Jesus who was not conscious of sin could accept baptism from John.

John, in short, emerges as an eschatological prophet: he proclaimed the imminence of the end, marked by fiery judgment. This is a distinctively apocalyptic view. In apocalyptic perspective there is, in our world, a war to the death between good and evil. Good will surely triumph. Evil, and all evildoers, will perish in final judgmental conflagration. Now is the time of decision. The tone of the Baptist's clarion call (in Matthew and Luke) is characteristic of apocalyptic: "You brood of vipers! Who warned you to flee from the wrath to come? ... Even now the axe is lying at the root of the trees ... every tree that does not bear good fruit is cut down and thrown into the fire ... His winnowing fork is in his hand ... the chaff he will burn with unquenchable fire" (Mt 3:10-12; see Lk 3:7-9). In Matthew (3:11-12) the agent of this fiery judgment is a coming one "who is more powerful" than the Baptist. In Mark 1:7-8 the "more powerful one" will (on the last day) baptize with the Holy Spirit, that is, wholly cleanse the repentant sinner. John does not specify who this "stronger one" is.

The evidence, from Josephus and the gospels (see Mt 11:2-19; Lk 7:18-35), substantiates the impression that John the Baptist, a Jewish prophet, had gained a reputation and a following. For very different reasons he attracted the attention of Herod Antipas and of Jesus of Nazareth. His ministry preceded that of Jesus – who indeed, for a time, became involved in it. And his movement did not end with his death but continued apart from the Christian movement (see Acts 18:24-19:7). John was worthy of the accolade of Jesus: "Truly I tell you, among those born of women no one has arisen greater than John the Baptist" (Mt 11:11; see Lk 7:28).

Disciple of the Baptist

The starting-point for any account of the ministry of Jesus of Nazareth is his encounter with John the Baptist: the call which Jesus heard when he was baptized by John and to which he responded. By submitting to baptism Jesus became, in effect, a disciple of the Baptist.[7] John had begun his mission in the wilderness (Lk 3:2) of Peraea, beyond the Jordan, appearing where Elijah had disappeared (2 Kgs 2) and forcing the question of his identity (Mk 1:6). A wilderness audience would consist of travellers on an established route; a receptive audience would be Galilean pilgrims – avoiding hostile Samaria in a roundabout way to Jerusalem (see Lk 9:51-53). Jesus, very likely, had heard of the eschatological prophet. Now, as a Galilean pilgrim, he encountered this strange and striking man, who wore a camel-hair cloak bound with a leather belt: an Elijah-figure. Jesus received baptism and stayed with John – as Elisha had become a disciple of Elijah. Later, some of John's disciples, whether or not at his instigation, transferred to Jesus (Jn 1:35-42).

Some statements in the fourth gospel imply much more than might appear at first sight. Take John 3:22-23 – "After this Jesus and his disciples went into the Judean countryside, and he spent some time there with them and baptized. John was also baptizing at Aenon near Salim [in Samaria]." We could take this to mean that John had sent Jesus into Judea while he had gone to the more challenging Samaria. That the ministry of Jesus involved baptism is explicit in 3:22 and 4:1 – "Now when Jesus had heard, 'Jesus is making and baptizing more disciples than John ...'" The observation reflects a later dispute as to the relative merits of John's and Jesus' baptisms. It is obvious that 4:2 – "although it was not Jesus himself but his dis-ciples who baptized –" is a maladroit redactional "correction." Evidently, the concern was to distance Jesus from the Baptist.

Later, John moved into Galilee, territory of Herod Antipas, and was promptly arrested. The observation in John 4:3 is significant: "[Jesus] left Judea and started back to Galilee." The Baptist had been silenced. Jesus moved in to take his place: *noblesse oblige*. What emerges from all this is that, at first, Jesus was disciple of, and in the line of, the Baptist. At some time there was a radical change. The point seems to have been reached with Jesus' welcome for sinners. Although he admired John, Jesus was to follow his own way. John was a prophet of doom who preached "a baptism of repentance for the forgiveness of sins" (Mk 1:4) – and we need to keep in mind that Jesus, too, baptized. On the other hand, Jesus proclaimed: "The kingdom of God has come near" (1:15). It is a matter of emphasis. Where John prophesied the judgment of God, Jesus prophesied the salvation of God. Hearing, in prison, of the activity of Jesus, a per-plexed John sent two of his disciples to investigate. Jesus' reply was: "Go and tell John what you have seen and heard: the blind receive their sight, the lame walk, the lepers are cleansed, the deaf hear, the dead are raised, the poor have good news brought to them" (Lk 7:22). One can read between the lines. John was being told that there was another prophetic message, another prophetic style. One might put it that John was in the line of Amos -- that prophet of unrelieved gloom. Jesus was in the line of Hosea, prophet of God's gracious love. We must not, however, overlook the fact that Jesus, like Hosea, also spoke words of warning.

The baptism of Jesus by John is certainly historical – note the embarrassment of Matthew 3:13-15. We look to the implication of it. In the first place, it indicated a fundamental change in Jesus' life: he became a disciple of the Baptist. He had come to know the eschatological message of John and showed, by his adherence, his basic acceptance of it. He submitted to John's baptism as a seal on his decision to change his manner of life. Hitherto, he had been a village carpenter; henceforth he would be proclaimer of the word. He would preach *metanoia*, a radical change of heart, in a wholehearted striving to renew Israel. The baptism launched him on a road that would eventually lead to the cross – though, surely, this prospect did not then appear on his horizon.

IV. THE MINISTRY

At some point Jesus, onetime disciple of John the Baptist, did strike out on his own. According to the general run of the gospel narratives, he was engaged during the early part of his ministry in three main types of activity:

– He was engaged upon a broad appeal to the public. His aim was to make people aware of the presence of God as an urgent reality and to invite their appropriate response. In this he echoed in some measure the clarion call of the Baptist.

– He set himself to minister to human need by healing the sick, exorcizing evil and awakening hope in those who had lost hope. And he sought to lead men and women into new life under the inspiration of a personal attachment to himself. By going about doing good he gave concrete shape to his message of the rule of God – of ultimate salvation.

– While his ministry cast him, in part, as teacher, his outlook and approach differentiated him from rabbinic Judaism. He challenged people to rethink their ideas and hopes, only to be branded a heretic. He censured his contemporaries, and, in particular, the religious authorities, for shrugging off God's warnings. In his mission, controversy was forced upon him.

Jesus did not come preaching a "new religion": he came to renew Israel. His call was for *metanoia*, a radical change of heart. He had come to summon Israel to become what God had wanted his people to be. He had caught up the urgent call of the Baptist and had made it his own. He was quite clear as to his goal: "I was sent only to the lost sheep of the house of Israel" (Mt 15:24; see 10:5-6). Inherent in Jesus' vision, however, was a dimension that, eventually, would no longer fit in the old wineskins.

Jesus began his mission with optimism. He did not start off with a vision of violent death at the end of the road. But, as his mission progressed, he had to come to terms with the reaction and opposition that forced him to reckon with, first, the possibility and, then, the probability, of a violent end. It is likely that the temptation stories, put before the start of the ministry by Matthew and Luke, really concern decisions faced at a later date. Certainly, Gethsemane and the anguished cry on the cross (Mk 14:32-42; 15:34) – hardly to be thought of as later Christian refinements – witness to the agony of decision and the depressing prospect of failure.

It is not surprising that, in the atmosphere of the day, Jesus might have been, in some measure, viewed as a messianic figure. Messianic pretensions were urged by the religious authorities in their action against Jesus. They badly needed to present him (to Pilate) as being a political threat; the political overtones of messianism would serve. It is, moreover, likely that Jesus' opponents may have understood him or his followers to claim that he was the Messiah. Jesus himself did not claim to be Messiah – nor did he ever deny the role. It is very likely that some of his followers thought him to be the Messiah. It is evident that, after the resurrection, Jesus was, by his followers, regularly called the Messiah – Jesus Christ (Messiah).

V. DEATH AND BURIAL

The ministry of Jesus ended in final conflict with religious and political authority. Jesus was condemned to death by Pilate. He was promptly scourged: a severe flogging was a normal prelude to crucifixion. Death by crucifixion was, and was intended to be, degrad-

ing. Even choice of the place of Jesus' execution was calculated
insult. Archaeology has shown that Golgotha, a disused quarry,
was, at that time, a refuse-dump. There was nothing of majesty
about the death of Jesus, no trace of glory. It was customary for the
condemned man to carry his cross beam. A certain Simon of Cyrene
was recruited to assist Jesus. It was Jewish custom, prompted by
Proverbs 31:6-7, to provide condemned victims with drugged wine;
Jesus did not take the wine. By custom, the clothes of the condemned, if of any value, fell to the executioners. A superscription
on the cross was in accordance with Roman practice. Mark has
Jesus crucified at the third hour (9 a.m.). He died at the ninth hour
(3 p.m.) (Mk 15:25, 34). Jesus had spent six hours in agony. Yet, his
death came surprisingly early; crucified victims normally lingered
much longer.

The disciples of Jesus (except for some women – and they stood
well apart from the scene) had fled at his arrest; it was left to another
to bury him. Joseph of Arimathea, a Sanhedrin member, was concerned to fulfil the Law – here that the body of one hanged (displayed) should not be left overnight on the tree (Dt 21:23). (In Mt
27:57 and Jn 19:38 Joseph is said to have been a disciple of Jesus – a
manifest later development.) Joseph was duly granted the corpse of
Jesus (Mk 15:42-46). It would be a hurried, dishonourable burial of
one sentenced to death on a charge of blasphemy. The body was not
anointed. It was simply wrapped in a shroud and placed in a niche
of the disused quarry that was Golgotha. A far cry, indeed, from the
royal burial of the fourth gospel (Jn 19:38-42). What matters is that
the burial, for all its finality, was not the end. 'He is going ahead of
you to Galilee …" (Mk 16:7).

CHAPTER 3

Prophet

*They were all filled with the Holy Spirit
and spoke the word of God with boldness.* (Acts 4:31).

In the biblical context a prophet is God's spokesperson: one called and sent to proclaim the word of God. Old Testament prophets were very conscious of the call and of the task. We see this clearly when we look to an Amos, a Hosea, an Isaiah, a Jeremiah. "The Lord took me from following the flock ... And the Lord said to me, 'Go, prophesy to my people Israel'" (Amos 7:15); "Then I heard the voice of the Lord, saying, 'Whom shall I send?' ... And I said, 'Here I am, send me!'" (Is 6:8); "Before I formed you in the womb I knew you ... I appointed you a prophet to the nations" (Jer 1:5). The call was a powerful summons; the task was challenging and formidable. There was need for commitment and courage. By and large, the prophetic word would not be heard. The task involved rejection and suffering – even death. Jeremiah is a poignant instance of the loneliness of the call: "Under the weight of your hand I sat alone" (Jer 15:17). The mysterious prophetical figure of Second Isaiah paid the price in vicarious suffering: "He was despised and rejected. He was wounded for our transgressions ... it was the will of the Lord to crush him with pain ... yet he bore the sin of many and made intercession for the transgressors" (Is 53:3-12).

John the Baptist was a prophet in the stern line of Amos, an eschatological prophet. He looked to an imminent end and judgment – and the definitive salvation of the just. He paid the ultimate price for his fidelity to the word. Jesus of Nazareth, one-time disciple of John, was a prophet who shared something of the eschatological expectation of the Baptist. In significant ways he differed from John. Christians saw him as "the more powerful one" spoken of by the Baptist. He, also, was rejected and put to death.

It is not superfluous to advert to possible misunderstanding of the terms "prophet" and "prophecy". In current language they carry the exclusive meaning of prediction. This is not at all the primary meaning in biblical usage. A biblical prophet – spokesperson of God – addressed, first and foremost, the contemporary situation. He tended to be an outspoken critic of the religious and political status quo. He was proclaimer of God's purpose for his people. A text in Acts of the Apostles may be adapted to characterize the prophetic style. The little Christian group is shown in prayer. They besought the Lord to "grant to your servants to speak your word with all boldness" (Acts 4:29). Their prayer was answered: "They were all filled with the Holy Spirit and spoke the word of God with boldness" (4:31). A prophet, in word and deed, spoke the word with boldness. This did involve a concern for the future. There was prediction, in its measure – but always in relation to the present. Any reference to the future had meaning for, and relevance for, the prophets' audience.

The message of Jesus, lived and spoken, was, he was convinced, of utmost urgency. Here we look to the prophet Jesus as perceived by the Christian eyes of Mark. If Jesus was prophet, he was also much else. Or, perhaps, one might put it that other features of his activity were facets of his prophetic role. At any rate, he emerges as teacher, healer, exorcist. And he is to be seen as Messiah and Son of God. He was, surely, the Suffering Servant.

PROCLAMATION

Now after John had been arrested (delivered up) Jesus came to Galilee, proclaiming the good news of God and saying, "the time is fulfilled, and the kingdom of God has come near; repent, and believe in the good news" (Mk 1:14-15).

Mark's first summary – summary statements are a feature of his style – opens the public ministry of Jesus and covers its initial phase. We have observed that Jesus was, initially, a disciple of John the Baptist. Mark's linkage of John's arrest with the emergence of Jesus may imply as much, but the evangelist does not make an issue of it. Instead, his opening words are ominous: "After John was arrested (lit. delivered up)." The fate of the Baptist was to be delivered up to his enemies (6:17-29) "according to the definitive plan and foreknowledge of God" (see Acts 2:23) – after a mysterious divine purpose. The Baptist was a type of the suffering Messiah (see Mk 9:11-13); the long shadow of the cross reached to the start of the gospel. Yet now began the preaching of "the good news of peace" and Mark's sentence, "the kingdom (reign) of God has come near; repent, and believe in the good news" is an admirable summing-up of the preaching and message of Jesus. Like the Baptist (Mk 1:4), Jesus called for thorough-going conversion. More urgently, he called on people to embrace the good news. The evangelist intended the words "believe in the good news" to be taken in the Christian sense of faith in the good news of salvation through Jesus Christ.

Jesus is here firmly cast as a prophet, issuing a challenge and an invitation. He had a burning concern for the renewal of the people of Israel as God's holy elect. He would not define the holiness of God's people in cultic terms. He redefined it in terms of wholeness. Where other contemporary Jewish groups were, in their various ways, exclusive, the Jesus movement was inclusive. His challenge and his invitation were to all. What Jesus claimed was that the decisive intervention of God expected for the end-time was, in some sort, happening in his ministry. The kingdom is here and now present in history in that the power of evil spirits is broken, sins are forgiven, sinners are gathered into God's friendship. The kingdom, though in its fullness still in the future, comes as a present offer, in actual gift, through the proclamation of the good news. But it arrives only on condition of the positive response of the hearer.

The kingdom of God

The precise phrase "kingdom of God" occurs once only in the Old Testament, in Wisdom 10:10. The expression was not current in Judaism at the time of Jesus and was not widely used by early Christians. "Kingdom of God" is found predominantly in the synoptics and then almost always on the lips of Jesus. It was evidently central to Jesus' proclamation. "The kingdom of God was simply Jesus' special and somewhat abstract way of speaking of God himself coming in power to manifest his definitive rule in the end time. God coming in power to rule in the end of time: that is the point of Jesus' phraseology."[8] And this is why "reign" or "rule" of God is a more satisfactory rendering of the Aramaic *malkutha di elaha*. "Kingdom of God" is, however, traditionally firmly in place.[9] Jesus spoke, in the main, of a future kingdom. In the Lord's Prayer he taught his disciples to pray that God's kingdom come – that God would come at the end to save his people (Mt 6:10; Lk 11:2). In Mt 8:11-12, Lk 13:28-29 Jesus spoke of many coming from east and west (Gentiles) to join Abraham and Isaac and Jacob at the glorious banquet in the kingdom of God. In Mark 14:25 (Lk 22:18) Jesus, in prophesying his imminent death, confidently saw himself at the table of that banquet – drinking new wine in the kingdom of God. And the beatitudes, in their Q form – see Lk 6:20-21 – ("Q" is the hypothetical common source of Matthew and Luke where they differ from Mark) have as their background God as vindicator of widows and orphans, as champion of the oppressed.

The great reversal would come to pass when God will reveal himself in power and glory. Jesus proposed no deadline. The Marcan statements, "Truly I tell you, there are some standing here who will not taste death until they see that the kingdom of God has come with power" (9:1), and "Truly, I tell you, this generation will not pass away until all things have taken place" (13:30), are creations of the early church. Jesus did proclaim a definitive coming of God's kingdom, but he made no attempt to pinpoint the time of its coming.

If assertion of future coming was dominant in Jesus' proclamation of the kingdom, there is evidence that he also spoke of the kingdom as in some sort already present in his own words and deeds. We have, for instance, the Lucan sayings: "If it is by the finger of God that I cast out demons, then the kingdom of God has come to you" (Lk 11:20; see Mt 12:28) and "the kingdom of God is among you" (Lk 17:21). There is, too, Mk 1:15: "the kingdom of God has come near." And Mk 2:18-20, on fasting, also intimates that in some manner the kingdom is already present: "The wedding guests cannot fast while the bridegroom is with them, can they? As long as they have the bridegroom with them they cannot fast."

When we have in mind the fact that the kingdom of God is not primarily a state or place, but rather the dynamic event of God coming in power to rule his people Israel in the end-time, it is not surprising that the precise relationship between the future and present kingdom is not specified. That is why Jesus can speak of the kingdom as both imminent and yet present. In Jesus' eyes his healings and exorcisms were part of the eschatological drama that was already underway and that God was about to bring to its conclusion. The important point is that Jesus deliberately chose to proclaim that the display of miraculous power throughout his ministry was a preliminary and partial realization of God's kingly rule.

Jesus began his mission by summoning disciples. The passage 1:16-20, with two parallel episodes (1:19-20; 2:13-14), was shaped by Mark to bring out the nature of Jesus' call and the nature of the Christian response; in short, to show what "following Jesus" means. We are shown that the sovereign call of Jesus evokes the response of those called, a free response as we learn in the episode of the one who could not bring himself to follow – the man "who had great possessions" (10:17-22). These fishermen leave all, nets, boat and father, to follow Jesus without hesitation. The decisive factor is the person of Jesus himself. In order to become a disciple of Jesus one does not need to be exceptional. What counts is not intellectual or moral aptitude but the gracious call of Jesus. It is the mighty, immediate impression of Jesus on Peter and his companions, reinforced by his personal word of call, that brought them into his following and made them his disciples. The whole episode is stylized, of course. Mark is not intent on describing a scene from the ministry of Jesus. Rather, he is concerned with the theological dimension of a typical call to discipleship.

The call of the Twelve (3:13-19) was a solemn moment. This is evident in 6:7-13. In that passage Mark carefully avoided the statement, present in Matthew and Luke, that the disciples proclaimed the kingdom of God. In Mark's perspective the Twelve had not understood the true nature of the kingdom – which is perceived only in the light of the death of Jesus. Like the Baptist (1:4) they "proclaimed that all should repent" (6:12). Here, in 3:13-19, the evangelist had the sending out of 6:7-13 in mind, but his vocabulary shows that he looked beyond it. The Greek words *apostellein*, "to send out", and *keryssein*, "to preach", are terms which the apostolic church used to describe its mission. Mark was conscious of the post-resurrection missionary situation. The Twelve were to preach and to do: the word of God is proclaimed in word and action together.

Prediction

Prediction of future events is, in restrained measure, a feature of prophecy; the prophet Jesus did speak of the future. The section 8:31-11:10 of Mark's gospel is dominated by prophecies of the passion (8:31; 9:30-32; 10:33-34), each in a different locale: Caesarea Philippi (8:27), Galilee (9:30), and on the way to Jerusalem (10:32). The first prediction, "The Son of Man must undergo great suffering, and be rejected by the elders, the chief priests, and the scribes, and be killed, and after three days rise again" (8:31), closely attached to Peter's confession (8:29-30) is, in effect, the title of the second part of the gospel which begins at this point and will reach a climax on Calvary (15:39). The opening words, "The Son of Man must undergo great suffering" (see 9:12) give the prediction in simple form; the rest of the verse has been coloured by the events and the details have been conformed to the traditional account of the Passion. To this extent the prediction (like the others) is a *vaticinium ex eventu*. The kernel of the second prediction (9:30-32) – "The Son of Man is to be betrayed [delivered up] into human hands" – is likely to be close to the form of the earliest passion-saying which underlay the developed versions of the three predictions. In Aramaic it would run something like: "God will (soon) deliver up the son of man to the sons of men."

The third and lengthiest prediction (10:33-34) corresponds very closely with the stages of the passion narrative in chapter 15. Mark had already presented Jerusalem as the centre of hostility to Jesus. Twice he has mentioned that hostile scribes, come from Jerusalem, had engaged in controversy with him (3:22; 7:1). This present journey is headed for a clash in Jerusalem with "the chief priests, the scribes, and the elders" (11:27-33). "Jesus was walking ahead of them" (10:32) – he knew where he was going and what fate awaited him in the city. Luke (9:51) has put it aptly: "When the days drew near for him to be taken up, he set his face to go to Jerusalem." The resolute bearing of Jesus as he led the way stirred the disciples with amazement and a sense of foreboding. As for Jesus himself, perhaps, again, Luke has put his finger on Mark's intent: "I must be on my way, because it is impossible for a prophet to be killed outside of Jerusalem" (Lk 13:33). After this, Mark's Gethsemane scene (Mk 14:32-42) will come as a surprise. It will come as comfort for all who strive to "follow" Jesus (see 8:34).

The centre of the farewell discourse (Mk 13) is the description, in typically apocalyptic terms, of the future parousia of the Son of Man (13:24-28). Then comes an answer to the implied question: How long until the parousia? The answer is firm: "Truly I tell you, this generation will not pass away until all these things have taken place" (v 30). This is wholly consistent with 9:1: "Truly I tell you, there are some standing here who will not taste death until they see the kingdom of God has come with power." Each saying is cast as a prophetic oracle and, doubtless, both are the utterance of first-generation Christian prophets. For Mark, they are word of the Lord. He has left us in no doubt as to his conviction. The parousia will occur in his own lifetime; at the very least, his generation will not have passed away before the end comes. His assurance was anchored in the authority of the words of Jesus (13:31). Mark was sure that in 9:1 and 13:30 he was being true to the Jesus who regarded his death and vindication as marking the end, with nothing else to wait for (see 14:25). But Mark will not specify day or hour, because he cannot (13:32). For that matter, not even the members of the heavenly court (the angels), not even the Son himself, know the precise date of the end – the Son and the angels who are the protagonists of the parousia (13:26-27). It remains the secret of the Father. While v 32 was, seemingly, understood by Mark as indicating that the exact date of the coming is not known, the saying, in itself, may well represent an authentic saying of Jesus. It is not easy to envisage a Christian prophet attributing ignorance to the Son of Man. And an acknowledgment by Jesus that he did not in fact know the time of the end would rule out his setting a deadline for the kingdom, and would also account for speculation about the end in the early church.

In the passage 14:1-25, Mark's concern in v 1 was to connect this farewell meal with the Passover; in v 14 he explicitly designates it a Passover meal. (In fact, the Last Supper was a solemn farewell meal – not a traditional passover meal.) His other and chief purpose was to highlight Jesus' foreknowledge and authority. Between preparation for the Supper and the Supper itself the evangelist intercalated the announcement-of-betrayal passage (vv 17-21). Jesus' opening words (v 18) echo Ps 41:9: "Even my bosom friend in whom I trusted, who ate of my bread, has lifted his heel against me." His words, "one who is eating with me ... dipping bread into the bowl with me", express the horror of treachery in the sacred setting of table fellowship. There was the added awfulness: it is one of the Twelve. Shattering though it be, betrayal was in accordance with the divine plan for the passion: "as it is written." But human responsibility was not thereby diminished. What was written was that the Son of Man "goes": death was accepted by Jesus himself. And, behind it all is a chastening admonishment to the reader. Mark has placed the betrayal episode in the setting of eucharistic table fellowship. The Christian must ask: "Is it I? – am I a betrayer of the Lord Jesus?" (see v 19). One is reminded of Paul in 1 Cor 11:28: "Examine yourselves, and only then eat of the bread and drink of the cup."

In the quotation from Zechariah one finds the key to Mk 14:27-28. After declaring, "strike the shepherd, that the sheep may be scattered" (Zech 13:7) the oracle goes on to declare that two-thirds of the shepherd-king's people will perish (13:8). The remnant will be refined and tested to become truly God's people (13:9). Jesus gives assurance that his community, too, though scattered following the fate of their shepherd, will be reconstituted by him. He looks beyond his death and promises that the scattered flock will be gathered together again. "After I am raised up, I will go before you to Galilee" (Mk 14:28). The phrase, "I will go before you" could be taken as "I will lead you" or "I will go there beforehand"; it is clear from 16:7 that Mark understood it in the latter sense: the disciples would meet Jesus again in Galilee. It would be a rebirth for them, a new beginning. "Galilee" will be, again, the area of mission – of universal mission (see 13:10). Finally, in Jesus' reply to the high priest's question (14:61) he acknowledged that he was the Messiah, the Son of the Blessed One, and added, "You will see the Son of Man seated at the right hand of the Power, and coming with the clouds of heaven" (Mk 14:62). Mark, with his "you will see" refers to the Christian perception of a Jesus with the Father through resurrection, and the Christian expectation of his parousia.

GESTURE

In the style of Old Testament prophets, the prophet Jesus, too, performed prophetic gestures whose purpose was to bolster the prophetic word. For Mark's readers the entry of Jesus into Jerusalem (Mk 11:1-11) had an obvious messianic significance. It is likely that the basic episode took place not at Passover but at a Feast of Dedication. Mark's narrative would suggest a modest affair: the immediate disciples and Jesus riding in their midst. Nothing would have looked more commonplace than a man riding on a donkey; and a group of pilgrims, waving branches and shouting acclamations from Ps 118, would not have occasioned a second glance at the feast of Dedication.

Yet, whatever others might have thought, Christians knew that this entry of Jesus into Jerusalem (as it is here presented), however unassuming in practice, was, symbolically, the solemn entry of the Messiah-King into his city. Jesus took the initiative: he would enter as the king of Zechariah 9:9 – where it is Yahweh, as divine warrior, who rides into Jerusalem. There is studied reticence in Mark's narrative. The text of Zech 9:9 is not quoted (see Mt 21:5); there are no "crowds" (Mt 21;90), no "multitude" (Lk 19:37,39); the people had not explicitly acclaimed Jesus as "Son of David" (see Mt 21:29) – though they had spread their cloaks and leafy branches for his passage.

The entry was Jesus' first messianic claim; only those with eyes to see would recognize it as such. It was an advent in humility, not glory. What was at stake, for Jesus, was the nature and manner of his messiahship. At this moment, come to the city that would soon witness his passion and death, he could manifest himself. He had not come as temporal ruler or with worldly pomp. He came as a religious figure, a prince of peace, "humble and riding on a donkey" (Zech 9:9). Mark's narrative in 11:11 is consistent with his modest presentation in 11:1-10 and may reflect what really happened, or something quite like it. Jesus entered the temple by himself ("he entered"), unobserved. The simple procession had petered out before the city gate. Jesus' "looking around" indicated a critical survey which set the stage for the following episode.

Cleansing the Temple

In 11:15-18 the prophetic gesture of Jesus, his "cleansing" of the Temple, symbolically disrupted the Temple's cultic life. He is depicted as driving out those who offered for sale animals and birds and other commodities needed for the sacrifices, the pilgrims who bought from them, and the money-changers who changed the Greek and Roman currency of the pilgrims into the Jewish and

Tyrian coinage in which alone the temple tax could be paid. He pro-
hibited the carrying of cultic vessels. It is inconceivable, particularly
so near Passover with its influx of pilgrims, that Jesus could really
have cleared the crowded temple courts and brought the whole
elaborate business to a standstill. His action, on a necessarily very
limited scale, was a prophetic gesture, and would have been recognized as such.

The motivation of his action is given in 11:17. It opens with Marcan
emphasis on the teaching of Jesus and runs into a quotation of Is
56:7 with an echo of Jer 7:11. It was God's intention that the Temple
should be a house of prayer "for all nations" – of special interest to
Mark. This had not been achieved because the Temple remained the
jealously-guarded preserve of Israel. Worse, the Temple and its cult
had become a "den of robbers" as Jer 7:8-11 makes plain. The
Temple and its service had become an escape-hatch: the Temple
cult, it was felt, would automatically win forgiveness of ill behaviour and bring about communion with God. The prophet Jesus was,
in this respect, emphatically in the line of Amos, Hosea and
Jeremiah (see Amos 4:4-5; 5:21-24; Hosea 5:1-2; 6:1-6; Jeremiah 7:1-
15; 26:1-19). In Jesus' view, because it was so abused, the Temple
cult had no longer any *raison d'être*. Its time had run out. The
prophetic gesture presaged what his death was to achieve (15:38;
see 13:2; 14:58; 15:29). The chief priests and the scribes heard the
message (see 11:28). They would not forget. They bided their time.
One might observe that with the inclusion of the theme of prayer
(11:22-25), Mark makes the point that for Jesus' disciples prayer
takes the place of temple worship and marks a turn from places and
practices that are no longer authentic.

In the kingdom of God

The saying of 14:25 – "Truly I tell you, I will never again drink of the
fruit of the vine until that day when I drink it new in the kingdom of
God" – is likely, in some form, to have been part of Mark's liturgical
tradition. It is, in essence, quite like the declaration in 1 Cor 11:26:
"For as often as you eat this bread and drink the cup, you proclaim
the Lord's death until he comes." As it stands in the Supper narrative, Jesus looks forward, beyond death, to the kingdom. As in the
predictions of the passion (8:31; 9:31; 10:33-34) death is not the last
word. Here Jesus looks, with sure hope, to the eschatological ban-

quet. His words also show a break: the close association, supremely marked by table fellowship, with his disciples was at an end. But by expressing to them his own serene expectation, he was assuring them of renewed communion in the kingdom; this point has been made explicitly by Matthew (26:29).

This is a saying that has all the signs of coming from Jesus: he was prophesying his approaching death. He looked failure in the face. Yet, he had confidence in God; his prophecy in 14:25 was a final cry of hope. John Meier observes:

> The basic observation of hope in this verse (see Lk 22:18) is utterly discontinuous with the christological, soteriological, and eschatological ideas of the early church ... Instead of saving anyone from death Jesus needs to be saved out of death himself, and only God can do that ... There is no hint of Jesus' death as atoning sacrifice, to say nothing of an explicit affirmation of his resurrection, exaltation, or parousia ... He is simply placed at the banquet table drinking wine; he is one of the saved, no more, no less ... If Mark 14:25 may be called a word of comfort, it is a word of comfort that Jesus speaks more to himself than to his disciples. In the face of failure and approaching death, Jesus consoles himself with the promise of ultimately being seated by God at the final banquet, despite the collapse of his mission in this present world. Thus, the focus of the saying is on Jesus' death as a sign of failure rather than of salvation, and on the coming of God's kingdom as the salvation of Jesus rather than the parousia of Jesus. This is simply not the christology, soteriology, and eschatology of the first generation of Christians, no matter what branch or stream of tradition we examine.[10]

We shall see how well this assessment squares with an evaluation of Gethsemane (14:32-42) and of Jesus' cry of Godforsakenness (15:34).

A prophet without honour (Mk 6:1-6a)

The episode of the rejection of Jesus at Nazareth (6:1-6a) had deep meaning for Mark and he placed it deliberately at this point in his gospel. A poignant problem in the early days of the church was the fact that while many Gentiles were responding to the good news, the Jewish people resisted it (see Rom 9-11). Already, in Mark, the bitter opposition of the authorities has been demonstrated (2:1-3:6) and Jesus was shown as misunderstood even by his own family (3:20-35). Now, at the close of the Galilean ministry, his own towns-people were challenged to make up their minds about his person and his claims, and they took offence at him. Their rejection of him was an anticipation of his rejection by the Jewish nation (15:11-15). That final rejection was possible because the blindness of people to God's revelation had been present from the start (see Jn 1:10-11). The issue is one of faith or unfaith in Jesus. Or, in Christian terms, faith in or rejection of the Lord.

The passage lays bare one of the roots of unbelief. Jesus' townsfolk reacted with initial surprise. They wondered at the origin ("where") of his wisdom; they had heard of his "deeds of power". They were on the verge of asking the right question about him. But they made the mistake of imagining that they already had the answers to their own questions. Besides, there was the scandal of Jesus' ordinari-ness: they could not bring themselves to acknowledge the greatness or the mission of a man who was one of themselves. They "took offence" at him: by Mark's day *skandalon* had practically become a technical term to designate the obstacle which some found in Christ and which blocked them from passing to Christian faith and disci-pleship (see Rom 9:32-33; 1 Cor 1:23; 1 Pet 2:8). The proverb of v 4 – "Prophets are not without honour, except in their hometown ...' – in some form, was current in the ancient world. Jesus implicitly assumed the role of prophet. His word must have consoled the early church in face of the enigmatic refusal of the chosen people as a whole to accept the message of Jesus. Christian communities down the ages would have done well to have taken it to heart. Prophets are never comfortable people to have about and we are adept at finding ways of discrediting them.

Rejection

"Jerusalem, Jerusalem, the city that kills the prophets, and stones those who are sent to it" (Lk 13:34; Mt 23:37).

It is the fate of a prophet to find oneself ignored, or repulsed, or worse. Jesus was no exception and, as we have seen, was conscious of it. Jesus had carried out his mission in Galilee: teaching, healing, exorcizing (Mk 1). Soon there was confrontation, documented in a series of five controversies (2:1-3:6). The series ends on a sinister note: "The Pharisees went out and immediately conspired with the Herodians against him, how to destroy him" (3:6). The odd association of Pharisees and Herodians (supporters of Herod Antipas) may be explained by the link between the Baptist and Jesus. The typical opponents of Jesus (Pharisees) joined with the supporters of the man who had John executed in a common plot to have Jesus put to death. Now we know that the hostility of the religious authorities – it was the Jerusalem priests who brought about the death of Jesus, but "Pharisees" will serve as the opponents – can have no other issue. Death, in Mark's story, looms as a dark cloud over the future course of Jesus' ministry.

His own received him not (3:20-35)

Mark's distinctive "sandwich" technique points us, unerringly, towards an understanding of the passage 3:20-35 – the episode of the scribes is sandwiched between the two sections on the family of Jesus (3:20-21, [22-30], 31-35). It is his pointer that "slices" and "filling" be taken as a unit. In v 21 the Nazareth family, concerned for Jesus, had come to "restrain" him. They wanted to put him away for his own good: "He has gone out of his mind." Then emerged "the scribes who came down from Jerusalem": official Jewish reaction; Jesus was under investigation. Verse 20 contains two accusations: he was possessed by Beelzebub, an evil spirit; his exorcisms were wrought "by the ruler of the demons", that is, Satan. These scribes had witnessed Jesus' healings; they had passed judgment. Like Job's comforters, they were complacently sure of the truth of their theology. Jesus was one who did not observe the sabbath, one who freely associated with sinners. His conduct was an affront to the holy God. Jesus' power – they could not deny the healings – was surely not from God. That left one other source! He was casting out the malign influences that caused sickness through the power of Satan – evil itself!

The accusations are taken up in turn in vv 28-29 and 27. The charge that Jesus cast out demons by the power of Satan was answered by denial that Satan was divided against himself. Can a divided kingdom stand firm? Can a dynasty, riven within, survive? And if Satan was suffering setbacks (the healings and exorcisms) might it not be that a power stronger than Satan was about? The explanatory editorial comment in v 30 – "for they said, 'He has an unclean spirit'" –

shows that the charge of blasphemy against the Holy Spirit (vv 28-29) is to be taken as Jesus' response to the accusation of being possessed. That comment makes clear that "blasphemy against the Holy Spirit" means the attribution of the exorcisms of Jesus (and, by implication, his whole ministry), wrought by the power of the Spirit, to a malign source. The "sin" or "blasphemy" is not so much an offence against the Spirit as humankind's refusal of the salvation which God was offering through the Spirit active in Jesus. The whole presence and ministry of Jesus made abundantly clear that, from God's side, there is no such thing as an unforgivable sin. The story obviously took for granted Jesus' reputation as an exorcist. Not the exorcisms, but the source of them, was questioned. Jesus was healer and exorcist as well as prophet.

The family was still about (3:31-32). Seated in the crowded house, Jesus was told that his mother and brothers were outside, wanting to speak with him – wanting to restrain him! (v 21). Too much had happened too quickly; Jesus was lost to them, and they sensed it. Jesus looked upon those who crowded around, hanging on his words. He had lost his natural family; but he had gained another family. His mother and brothers and sisters were not outside – they were right there before him. Those who hear and do the will of the Abba are, now and always, Jesus' brother and sister and mother – the faithful women and men of God (vv 33-35).

The beloved Son (12:1-12)

The allegorical features of the parable of the Wicked Tenants (12:1-12) are evident: the vineyard is Israel, the owner is God, the maltreated servants are God's messengers to Israel, notably the prophets, the beloved son is Jesus. In Mark's setting the parable is one of five controversy stories (11:27-12:37). "Then he began to speak to them in parables" (12:1) – "they" are the chief priests, scribes and elders (see 11:27; 12:12). The Old Testament has a notable instance of a prophet employing a parable with dramatic effect: Nathan's entrapment of David (2 Sam 12:1-7). Mark's parable, too, is dramatic. The description and equipping of the vineyard (Mk 12:1) are based on the allegory of Is 5:1-7 which represents Israel as vineyard of the Lord. Mark's significant modification is to have the landlord let out his vineyard to tenants. It follows that failure is not on the part of the vineyard (the people) as in Isaiah; the failure is of the tenants, the leaders of the people.

The landlord sent his servants to collect his rent, only to have them insulted and maltreated, even killed. He decided to play his last card. He had a beloved son, his only son. He would send him: "Surely, they will respect my son!" But they killed him and, contemptuously, left him unburied (vv 6-8). So had God dealt with an obdurate people, sending to them, time and again, his servants the prophets. And now, supreme graciousness, he has sent his only Son. This was the ultimate challenge. But the tenants, the leaders, did away with him. Jesus' rhetorical question in v 9 – "What will the owner of the vineyard do?" – gives punch to the parable; his reply points to judgment on faithless Israel. The tenants, leaders of the covenant people, have brought upon themselves their own dismissal; they have rejected the Son of God (v 9). God looks to others; Mark, likely, has the Gentiles in mind. The parable is aptly in place after 11:12-21 (prophetic gestures aimed at the Temple) and after the question about Jesus' authority (11:27-33).

And when there is question of the alleged rejection of Israel, one must keep in mind the conviction of Paul who, after all, as a fellow Jew, had special affinity with Jesus of Nazareth, that "all Israel will be saved" (Rom 1:26). Why? On the basis of an impeccable biblical argument: "The gifts and the calling of God are irrevocable" (11:29).

It is a matter of supreme importance that this parable appears in all three synoptic gospels shortly before their passion narratives. It is a wholly clear indication of how they understood "he did not spare his own Son." The Father had not thrown his Son to the wolves. The Father had not wished the death of his Son. Father and Son had delivered themselves to the humans they would save. Jesus did not die – Jesus was killed. It was not the Father who killed Jesus.

With the quotation of Ps 118:22-23 in vv 10-11, the figure passes from vineyard to that of building: God's rejected Son has become the cornerstone, the foundation, of the new community. Mark's readers can take heart; they are stones in a building raised by God himself with Jesus Christ as chief cornerstone (see Eph 2:19-22). In his conclusion (v 12) Mark typically distinguished between the hostile teachers of Israel and the common people who were sympathetic to Jesus (see 11:18). The leaders had caught the drift of the parable only too well (v 12) – "When they realized that he had told this parable against them, they wanted to arrest him, but they

feared the crowd". They remained "those outside" (4:11) because
they rejected its challenge. They could not bring themselves to
acknowledge Jesus. They had rejected the prophet. Now they must
silence him.

CONCLUSION

Jesus of Nazareth had responded to the challenge of an uncompromising prophet: John the Baptist. He became a prophet in his turn
and began to proclaim the good news of the rule of God. Soon, God
would come in power, bringing about the great reversal. But one
did not wait, passively, for it to happen. There must be human
openness and human response. Besides, the rule of God was already
present – present in Jesus, in his words and deeds. It could not be
otherwise: in Jesus God was present and active. Besides, he, as
prophet, had been sent. After remarkable success at Capernaum
(1:21-34) Jesus had gone to pray (1:35), and Simon and his companions
"hunted for him" (1:36). They felt that he, the wonder-worker and
healer (vv 32-34), was missing a great opportunity. Jesus would not
be turned from his prophetic task of proclaiming the kingdom
(1:14). "For that is what I came out to do" (v 38): he explained to his
disciples that he must not linger to satisfy the curiosity of the people of Capernaum. Luke had correctly caught the Marcan nuance
when he wrote: "for I was sent for this purpose" (Lk 4:43), that is,
sent by the Father. The kernel of his prophetic message was: the
kingdom of God has come near.

God's rule becomes real only when it finds expression in human
life. It found expression in the life of Jesus. He "went about, doing
good"; he championed the outcast; he welcomed sinners. Jesus, in
his own lifestyle, gave concrete expression to the good life – a life
worthy of humankind. It is up to us, his disciples, in our different
and greatly changed world, to give expression – in our turn – to the
good life. It is our task to give the kingdom flesh and blood in our
world. Of course, the kingdom which would emerge if God's rule
were to hold sway would be very different from any existing political
entity and different, too, from any religious structure then and since.

The kingdom can be a reality only at the cost of wholehearted conversion. It is the charism of a prophet to see to the heart of things.
Only the starkest words can match his uncomplicated vision. The

genuine prophet will speak a message of comfort, based on the faithfulness of God, but it will never be a comfortable message. That is why the demands of Jesus were uncompromising. He knew, better than any other, that sin was the greatest evil, the ultimate slavery. He discerned sin in selfishness and greed, in the seeking of status – most reprehensibly in the seeking of ecclesiastical power and privilege. He was conscious of sinful structures, political and religious. Indeed, he turned authority upside down (Mk 10:42-45). He took his stand on the Fatherhood/Motherhood of God. He believed that all men and women are children of this Parent, that all are sisters and brothers. He regarded sin as whatever conflicts with that family relationship of respect and love. Logically, then, his prophetic message was "good news for the poor'. The poor were victims of the oppressive power of sin, an oppression mediated through sinful structures. This concern of Old Testament prophets found fresh urgency in Jesus' preaching.

In preaching the rule of God, Jesus was defining God. He proclaimed a God bent on the salvation of humankind. That is why he announced good news to the poor – the needy of every sort, the outcast. That is why he was friend of sinners, why he had table fellowship with them. And, in the long run, it was because Jesus had proclaimed a God of overwhelming mercy that he ended up on a cross. That God was unacceptable to the religious people of his day. That God is unacceptable to the professional religious of any day.

Jesus was aware of the fate of prophets; he suffered the fate of a prophet. He was rejected. He was put to death. By the standard of the world he was a failure. True, he had got off to a promising start in his acknowledged task of renewing Israel and he had won a heartening response. But opposition began to emerge almost from the start. As Peter showed at Caesarea Philippi, those who began to pin vague or explicit messianic expectations on him quickly became disillusioned – what was all this about suffering and death? (Mk 8:27-33). The poignant words of the Emmaus disciples are eloquent: "We had hoped that he was the one to redeem Israel!" (Lk 24:21) – they had been let down with a bang.

Failure is an unavoidable factor of our human existence. While there is failure that is blameworthy, there is much failure beyond our control. Surely, it would be comfort, in our season of failure, to know that Jesus, too, – like Jeremiah – had had a real experience of failure. We recall the consoling words of Hebrews: "Because he himself was tested by what he suffered, he is able to help those who are being tested" (Heb 2:18). Surely it is heartening, in the dejection of failure, to hear in the silence of prayer, the gentle, reassuring words: "My sister, my brother, I, too, knew the agony of failure." To hear these words we must first be prepared to acknowledge a Jesus who could fail. If our christology will not allow for that – then he can he no help to us in our times of failure. The christology of Mark allows for it. The Jesus of Mark, as prophet sent by God, fulfilled the role of the Servant (Is 52:13-53:12). We need to know the Jesus of Mark and the ultimate promise of the cross: the triumph of failure. In Jesus God's victory has been won: on the cross. Hence, the Christian paradox: the victim is the victor.

CHAPTER 4

Teacher

They were astounded at his teaching,
for he taught them as one having authority,
and not as the scribes (Mk 1:22).

While Mark gives, in comparison with Matthew and Luke, little of
the teaching of Jesus – but more than is regularly acknowledged –
he does insist, firmly, on the teaching activity of Jesus. If Jesus were,
undoubtedly, prophet, he stood too in the line of Old Testament
wisdom teachers. On the first sabbath of his ministry Jesus taught
in the Capernaum synagogue (Mk 1:21). Later, in a house, he continued to "speak the word" to the people of the town (2:2) and he
taught crowds gathered by the sea of Galilee (2:13; 4:1). He taught,
this time without success, in his Nazareth synagogue (6:2). At first,
however, his hearers spontaneously recognized the significance of
his presence: "Where did this man get all this? What is this wisdom
that has been given to him?" He was, it must have seemed, purport-
ing to be a wisdom-teacher. And, when a great crowd followed him
to a desert place, his first concern was that they lacked a teacher;
they were like sheep without a shepherd, "and he began to teach
them many things" (6:34). His teaching – and we have only a select-
ion – covered a wide range.

PARABLES

He spoke in parables

Jesus taught, strikingly, in parables. We associate parable so closely
with him indeed that it might seem as though he had created the
parable. Rather, he made brilliant use of a genre which was already
of long tradition. The Greek word *parabolé* means a juxtaposition or
comparison of two realities. In classical rhetoric, the strict parable
had only one point of reference and might be described as an
extended simile. According to Aristotle, parables are of two kinds:

true events taken from history, and the imaginatively fictional. His preference was for the first sort. In the Old Testament, however, the context is history, and the imaginative parable abounds. Jesus, and the New Testament writers, followed the Bible, not Aristotle. The Old Testament, then, is the proper background of gospel parable study.[11]

Mashal

The Septuagint translators (the Septuagint is the pre-Christian Greek version of the Hebrew Scripture) had lit on *parabolé* as their preferred rendering of the Hebrew *mashal*; for them, the Greek term took on the wide-ranging meaning of *mashal*. That can be: a representation or a type, a simile or a metaphor, a maxim or a pithy saying, a symbol or a riddle. It might carry, also, the aura of a "dark saying", implying mystery. The bewildering range of meaning may be gauged from the fact that each proverb in the book of Proverbs – two-line couplets in the main – is a *mashal* (e.g. Prov 10:1), while each of the elaborate speeches of Job is also termed *mashal* (e.g. Job 29:1) In the gospels the term *parabolé* includes not only parable but aphorism – a pithy, arresting saying, complete in itself, e.g. 'The sabbath was made for humankind, and not humankind for the sabbath' (Mk 2:27). Both parable and aphorism invite reflection and can be more challenging and effective than straightforward statements.

By Jesus' day the parable had become a familiar form in rabbinical preaching. It had a history, as witness Nathan's clever parable in 2 Samuel 12:1-4 – with a hapless David toppling into the parabolic trap (12:5-7). In general, biblical parable drew material from daily life and followed set meanings: vineyard, sons, servants represented Israel, king or father meant God, feast indicated the messianic age, harvest, the judgment. When Jesus chose to speak in parables he was following a convention familiar to his hearers.

It has long been scholarly practice to take the gospel parables out of their settings in order to deal with them as a genre on their own. But, surely, it is right to insist that parables ought to be studied in their one sure *Sitz im Leben* – the place of each parable in a particular gospel. A gospel parable can be rightly understood in its gospel context. It is not possible confidently to situate any parable in the historical ministry of Jesus. One cannot really get back there. But each parable does appear at a particular place in each gospel. We can recognize its literary setting and ask what it is doing just there. One is not thereby suggesting that the gospel setting of a parable exhausts the potential of its challenge.

Parables in Mark

In chapter 4 of Mark (precisely, Mk 4:1-34) we have a collection of parables and, in vv 10-12, the evangelist's theory of the purpose of parables. No treatment of gospel parables can avoid trying to come to terms with the implication of Mk 4:10-12. On the face of it, one is told that Jesus spoke in parables in order that his hearers should not understand. That such might have been his purpose is so alien to the character of Jesus as to be incredible. We must look to the evangelist for an explanation. It is already instructive that Matthew (13:10-17) has notably tailored Mark's text to his purpose. He has distinguished between a time when Jesus had spoken openly to "the Jews" and a time when, in reaction to their rejection of him, he reverted to parabolic teaching. Each in his manner, Matthew and Mark were facing up to a problem which exercized the early church: the obduracy of Israel (see Rom 9-11).

Mark, for his part, seems to have taken a staunchly deterministic approach: there are those who, divinely enlightened, understand and accept the message of the parables, while "those outside" fatally misunderstand and reject. In Mark's parable theory passage the Isaian text (Is 6:9-10) is perfectly in place: unreceptivity is presented as something foreseen, even ordained, by God. Besides, there is the esoteric facet of a parable. In Mark, while parables are spoken in public (see 4:3-34) their meaning is (in theory) grasped only within the inner circle of disciples. This is particularly suited to Mark's gospel with its emphasis on the mysterious nature of Jesus.

In its Isaian setting the declaration Is 6:9-10 is a forceful and paradoxical way of proclaiming what is inevitably going to happen: the prophet's preaching will not be heeded. In the Marcan text the evangelist is addressing the obduracy of Israel. Why did, by and large, the Jewish contemporaries of Jesus not hearken to his message, not come to understand him? And why did the Jewish people continue to resist the preaching of Mark's community? Mark's

answer is stark: their rejection of the gospel was within God's plan.
Nor is he alone in this view. Early Christian thinkers tended to
account for the rejection of the message of Jesus and of the apostles
by asserting that such was the will of God (see Rom 9:18-19; 10:16-
21; 11:7-10; Jn 12:37-41; Acts 28:25-28). They were influenced by a
currently accepted apocalytic view of a deterministic will of God.
Mark's distinctive contribution was to exploit the mysterious
aspect of parable in that direction. Ultimately he was, in tortuous
fashion, asserting that Israel's inexplicable behaviour had a divine
purpose. It was Paul's conviction also, expressed in an equally tortuous manner (Rom 9-11). Of course the New Testament writers,
like their Old Testament predecessors, maintained that people
carry responsibility for their actions, and this responsibility was not
taken to be voided by the apocalyptic doctrine of determinism. In
accord with this belief in a deterministic will of God, Mark proposed that Jesus had taught in mysterious parables; to the disciples
alone was revealed the secret of the kingdom (4:11). Through them
his teaching would be preserved and passed on. Yet, Mark will go
out of his way to insist that the disciples did not comprehend Jesus
and did not grasp his teaching. His statement that God had granted
the secret (mystery) of the kingdom to some while hiding it from
others relates to the situation of his day and looks beyond the specific problem of official Jewish rejection of Jesus and of the good
news. He had in mind the situation illustrated in the explanation of
the parable of the Sower (4:14-20). His point was that for all those
whose "hardness of heart", whose resistance to the good news, placed
a barrier to the invitation and challenge of Jesus, the parables were
riddles to which they had no key. He was sure that God alone could
open hearts to the word and bring it to harvest. All of this is the
viewpoint of the Marcan Jesus, that is to say, of the evangelist himself.

Sower and explanation (Mk 4:1-9, 13-20)

The text of the parable of the Sower (4:1-9) is notably Semitic and
the lines of it are simple and clear. But because we can no longer
determine its setting in the ministry of Jesus we cannot be sure of its
original meaning. It is commonly taken to be a parable of the kingdom; it is not at all clear that it was ever meant to be such. What is
beyond doubt is that, for Mark, it is a parable of the word; it is quite

likely that this, too, was Jesus' intent. There is notable emphasis on hearing: "Listen!" (v 3), "Let anyone with ears to hear listen!" (v 9), an emphasis sustained throughout the parable passage. It surely cannot be claimed that Mark had turned the parable from its original purpose. On the other hand, the parable might be characterized as a parable of the soils; it is where the seed falls and what happens to it that are decisive.

Structurally, the parable of the Sower falls into two parts: the first part (vv 4-7) is negative – the grain and seedlings and young plants perish; the second (v 8) is positive – the rest of the grain flourishes and the yield is startling. "Listen" (v 3) echoes the "Hear" of Dt 6:4. For Mark the admonition highlighted, from the outset, the importance, throughout this narrative, of "hearing" (see v 9) and also suggested that parables were meant to provoke thought. The farmer sowed haphazardly: on the path, on rocks, among thorns (the incongruous, a feature of several parables) – also happily, on fertile soil. The story had something more than farming in mind. The parable was about the hearers of the word – the different soils. The parable is allegory as its explanation (vv 14-20) insists. Its main concern is the word and the hearers of the word. The hearer is exhorted to receive the word in faith and keep it with steadfastness. And the "word" was not only Jesus' proclamation of the coming kingdom but, more immediately for Mark, the proclamation of the Christian message. Here, too, is the counter to the determinism of vv 11-12, stressing human responsibility and the need for a response to the proclamation. The question of Jesus in v 13 points to another dimension of the parable: it is the key to understanding all other parables. It is so because it is concerned with the presupposition of all parables, the word sown by Jesus. It is, then, a parable not only on the hearing of the word but on the right hearing of parables.

The explanation of the Sower (vv 14-20) is a commentary which takes up and explains each phrase of the parable. Its language shows it to be a product of the early church which reflects the missionary experience of early Christians. Noteworthy is the attention to the various types of soil. But this was already a feature of the parable. The explanation builds on what was already there; it does not give a new and different twist. The seed is the gospel preaching. This word is sown in the hearers; it is "seeded" in them. Four categories of hearers are distinguished in terms of where the seed had fallen: "on the path", "on rocky ground", "among the thorns" and on "the good soil". The fate of the word was different in each case.

The explanation is there because Christians had, perforce, to acknowledge that few had really taken to heart Jesus' word. They asked the question: Why such a gulf between them and those who would not see? They found an answer in this parable. How could they have expected it to be otherwise? Think of what happens when the sower scatters his seed. Not every seed bears fruit. Much is lost for one reason or another. This understanding then led them to delineate the forms of resistance to the word. Many people were like those on the path: the word did not reach them, as though the devil had swiped it away at the very moment of receiving. Or, many people seemed like shallow growth: they are ready to receive, but were unable to persevere. Or, many people were like seed under thorns: they heard, but the word lost its significance because they were choked by cares and distractions. The major concern of the explanation was the structure of human life itself. The shallow mind, the hard heart, worldly preoccupation, persecution – these were precisely the obstacles which frustrated the growth of faith. The explanation presupposed a period when Christian faith was tested by such factors. It offered warning and encouragement. And Mark presented it as a word of Jesus.

Other Marcan parables

The parable of the Seed Growing to Harvest (4:26-29) is proper to Mark. It seems best to take it as a parable of contrast between the inactivity of the sower (after the initial sowing) and the certainty of harvest. The sower goes his way; the seed sprouts and grows without him taking anxious thought. It is God who brings about the growth of the kingdom. Paul had learned the lesson of the parable: "I planted, Apollos watered, but God gave the growth" (1 Cor 3:6). It may be that, originally, it was Jesus' reply to those who looked, impatiently, for a forceful intervention of God; or it may have been meant to give assurance to those of the disciples who had become discouraged because little seemed to be happening. Mark surely takes it in the latter sense. Jesus encouraged his disciples: in spite of hindrance and apathy the seed was being sown. Its growth is the work of God who will bring it to harvest.

The parable of the Mustard Seed (4:30-32) is another parable of contrast; but again the idea of growth must be given due weight.
Contrast between insignificant beginning and mighty acheivement
is primary – but the seed does grow into a plant. The detail of
branches in which birds nest (v 32) manifestly recalls Ezek 17:23. In
Mark's view, the proclamation of the kingdom will bring all
nations within its scope (see 13:10). The parable would have been
the reply of Jesus to an objection, latent or expressed: could the
kingdom really grow from such inauspicious beginnings? His reply
was that the little cell of disciples would indeed become a kingdom.
And, in the last analysis, if the kingdom does reach its full dimension, that is not due to anything in the men and women who are the
seed of the kingdom; the growth is due solely to the power of God.
After all, the "kingdom" is nothing other than the saving presence
of God. This is why Jesus could speak with utter confidence of the
final stage of the kingdom. And that is why both parables are a call
for openness and for patience.

The Beloved Son (12:1-12). See above, p. 44-46

The Doorkeeper (13:33-37)

In the farewell discourse (Mark 13), after the comforting presentation of the parousia (13:24-27), Mark protracts the note of encouragement by stressing the nearness of the parousia. But he insisted
that the intervening time be spent in watchfulness. True to his
understanding of discipleship, outlined in chapters 8-10, there
could be no room for complacency in the life of the Christain. The
parable of the Doorkeeper (13:33-37), as Mark found it, had already
passed through a process of reshaping. The main sentence,
"Therefore, keep awake ... or else he may find you asleep when he
comes suddenly" is the application of the parable. Significantly, it is
"the master of the house" who will return, not the "man" of v 34: it
is Christ himself. The parable is now understood in christological
terms. Christ is the departing Lord and the parousia will mark his
return.

DISCIPLESHIP

Christians may be children of God but they are truly such only on
condition that they understand what it means and live with its
demands. Mark's own understanding of discipleship was the same

as that of Paul: "If children, then heirs, heirs of God and joint heirs with Christ – if, in fact, we suffer with him so that we may also be glorified with him" (Rm 8:17). His preoccupation with discipleship follows hard on his concern with christology. The way of discipleship had been firmly traced by Jesus himself. "If any want to become my followers, let them deny themselves and take up their cross and follow me" (8:34). For Mark there is no other way of discipleship. Following the pattern of the victory of Christ, the Christian is not preserved from suffering and even death, but is sustained through suffering and death.

True discipleship (8:34-9:1)

Coming directly after the first prediction of the passion (8:31-33), the passage 8:34-9:1 asserts, unequivocally, that the disciples of the Son of Man (v 31) must necessarily walk in his path. Jesus had "called the crowd with his disciples" (v 34): this challenge was addressed to all. Discipleship is costly, and one may be tempted to shrink from what it entails. The loyal disciple would not be preoccupied with personal interests but would follow in sustained faithfulness to Jesus. The way of discipleship is not easy and one may be tempted to shrink from what it entails. To seek thus to evade risk and save one's life – to have things one's own way – would be to suffer the loss of one's true self. One prepared and willing to risk all for Jesus and for the good news is one who will achieve authentic selfhood. If human life on earth is so much more precious than anything else in creation, if no one can put a price on it, how much more precious the eternal life to be won by the faithful disciple. There is the challenge. A warning sounds for one who would not follow, for one who would draw back, ashamed of the Way, one who would seek to save one's life (see 4:14-19). Jesus, too, the warning rings, will be ashamed of such a one, will not acknowledge such a one, when he will reappear in glory at the end (8:38). And his return will not be long delayed. Already, in this generation, God's reign will be manifest in power. It is impossible for us to gauge what such conviction meant for Mark and his community. What is undeniable is that Mark was still certain that a Christian had to come to terms with the cross. Once this had been grasped, one had to spread the good news (see 13:10).

Mark assuredly looked beyond the ministry of Jesus. Like the author of Revelation, his concern was for the persecuted community of his day (see 13:9-13) – though, in neither case, was it yet all-out persecution. He reminded those followers of a rejected and cruci-fied Messiah that it should not surprise that they, too, were called upon to suffer. The cross had turned the values of the world upside down – it is indeed "a stumbling block" and "foolishness" (see 1 Cor 1:23). They must be steadfast in face of persecution. They must not be ashamed of Jesus' way of humiliation and suffering and death, if they do not want the glorious Son of Man to be ashamed of them at his coming. And they hear his comforting assurance, "Surely, I am coming soon" (Rev 22:20; see Mk 9:1).

True greatness (9:33-37).

The second prediction of the passion (9:30-32) is followed by fur-ther instruction on discipleship. It was needed because in vv 33-34 the disciples' lack of understanding was blatant. They, disciples of a master so soon to suffer bitter humiliation and death, are all too humanly involved in petty squabbling over precedence. The Teacher took his seat and called the Twelve to him. His message was unequivocal: "Whoever wants to be first must be last of all and servant of all" (v 35). He backed up his word with a prophetic ges-ture: the presentation of a little child. The manner of it tells much of the delicate sensitivity of Jesus: "taking it in his arms" – a touch proper to Mark (see 10:16). "Whoever welcomes one such child in my name welcomes me ..." (v 37). "Welcome" means loving service of the weaker members of the community, those who stand in greatest need of being served. A Christian is one baptized "into the name of" Jesus (Mt 28:19; 1 Cor 1:13, 15), so becoming his. That is why one meets (serves) Christ himself in the disciple and meets the Father in Christ. This is the dignity of Christian service. Mark has made the point that the revelation of Jesus cannot be acknowledged by one who is not ready to enter into the spirit of discipleship and thereby become "last" and "servant". One would hope that the Christian of today is attuned to the unambiguous message of this word of Jesus: greatness in his church is found in *diakonia*, service, and only there. A first step is to have discerned this. It is the right of the people of God to have such service. It is their right to demand that leadership in the church, at every level, be service, not in word, but in deed.

It is not so among you (10:35-45)

The third is the most detailed prediction of the passion in this gospel (Mk 10:33-34). Sadly, its stark words fell on ears deafened by selfish ambition (10:35-37). Jesus had asked of one who would follow him a readiness to face and share his sufferings. Now the request of the brothers James and John is naïvely direct: the first places in Jesus' messianic kingdom no less! When Jesus asked them whether they had considered the price to be paid for a share in his glory they responded with brash confidence (v 39). The power of the risen Lord would in due course break through the self-interest of James and John and give backbone to their facile enthusiasm; they will indeed courageously walk in the way of their Master. We may well find something of ourselves in this pair.

The other ten were no less uncomprehending than James and John; they were indignant at being circumvented by the shrewd pair (v 41). This was an appropriate occasion for another telling lesson in discipleship (vv 42-45). Jesus solemnly asserted that, in the community of his disciples, there is no place for ambition. His church is a human society: there is place for authority, for leaders. But those who lead will serve their brothers and sisters: the spirit of authority is *diakonia*. Surely Jesus had intended the paradox and had asked for it to be taken seriously. He first outlined the accepted standard of civil authority: domination, with rulers lording it over their subjects, making their presence felt in all areas of life (10:42). Then (v 43) he asserted that this was not, positively not, to be the pattern for those who professed to follow him. Jesus stood authority on its head. Greatness would be measuerd by service: the leader will be slave (*doulos*) of the community. There could be no place at all for styles and trappings and exercize of authority after the model of civil powers and princes. Is there anything in the gospels quite as categorical as this demand?

> You know that among the Gentiles those whom they recognize as their rulers lord it over them, and their great ones are tyrants over them. But it is not so among you; but whoever wishes to become great among you must be your servant, and whoever wishes to be first among you must be slave of all (Mk 10:42-44).

Where are we, today, in our church? Where, now, is the collegiality urged by Vatican II? Sooner or later – sooner rather than later – we must find the honesty to acknowledge that we have not hearkened to this word of the Lord. We must give ear to the prophetic word that challenges every abuse of authority. Otherwise, authority itself will be fatally compromised. People today will welcome leadership. They reject dictatorship.

The ground of the paradoxical behavior required of disciples is to be found in the example of the Son of Man (v 45). Here this distinctive authority (*exousia*) with its firm stamp of *diakonia* (service) is given christological underpinning. The saying – "For the Son of Man came not to be served but to serve, and to give his life a ransom for many" – specifies in what sense Jesus would "serve" people: he would give his life for them. *Lytron* ("ransom") was originally a commercial term; the ransom is the price that must be paid to redeem a pledge, to recover a pawned object, or to free a slave. In the Septuagint the term is predicated metaphorically of God who is frequently said to have bought, acquired, ransomed his people (e.g. Ps 49:8; Is 63:4). In its Marcan form the saying is related to Is 53:10-11 and "ransom" is to be understood in the sense of the Hebrew word *asham* of Is 53:10, an "offering for sin", an atonement offering. By laying down his life for a humankind enslaved to sin, Jesus fulfilled the word about the Servant in Is 53:10-11. Jesus had paid the universal debt: he gave his life to redeem all others. But this is metaphor, not crude commerce. The death of Jesus, in the Father's purpose and in the Son's acceptance, was gesture of sheer love: "Surely, they will respect my Son... not what I want, but what you want" (Mk 12:6; 14:36). Any suggestion that the death of the Son was the literal payment of a debt, the placating of an offended God, is blasphemy – though it has been a tragic misperception of Christians. God is ever motivated by love, not "justice".

This word of Jesus was clear. Would it be heard? Not throughout Christian history. But it was heard in the Jerusalem of Jesus' day, and heard by the Roman power, heard as subversive of authority. Jesus was dangerous and had to be silenced. His teaching was political dynamite.

The First Commandment (12:28-34)

Jesus' ideal of authority can thrive only in a context of *agapé*, "love". The centrality of love is asserted in the pronouncement story of 12:28-34. Jesus offers his answer to the question, "Which commandment is the first of all?" (v 28). It was a question the rabbis sought to answer. They looked for a commandment that outweighed all others, one that might be regarded as a basic principle on which the whole law was grounded. Because this scribe's question was an honest question by one well-disposed (vv 32-34), Jesus answered directly. He began by quoting the opening formula of the Shema , "Hear, O Israel: the Lord our God, the Lord is one: you shall love the Lord your God", and linked it with Lev 19:18 on the love of neighbour, "You shall love your neighbour as yourself". He had been asked to name the first commandment; he responded by naming two commandments. That is because, for him, the one followed directly and necessarily from the other. Love for neighbour arises out of love for God. He had taken and welded the two precepts. This seems to be original with Jesus. Insistence on love of neighbour here and now is another unmistakable indication that Jesus' eschatological vision had place for life in the present. For that matter, life in the present would determine one's eschatological future.

The scribe's reply (vv 32-33) is proper to Mark. He had agreed wholly with Jesus' answer and further specified that true love of God and loving service of others were more important than elaborate cult. His insistence on love with the whole heart was a recognition that love cannot be measured. Love is incompatible with a legalism that sets limits, that specifies meticulously what one must do and must avoid. Jesus' assurance that this scribe was not far from the kingdom of God was in truth an invitation. And we sense that, this time, the invitation will not be in vain (see 10:17-23). Nowhere else in the gospels does a scribe emerge in such a favourable light.

Legalism (7:1-22)

The controversy setting in 7:1-2 is similar to that in 2:8 and 2:23-24. From chapter 5 on Mark has displayed interest in the Gentile mission; we can appreciate that the matter of Jewish observance was an issue for his community. "The scribes who had come from Jerusalem" (see 3:2) represent the Jewish position. The question to be answered was whether Gentile Christians had to conform to Jewish tradition (see Gal 2; Acts 15). Mark's adaptation of the Jesus tradition served his situation.

As the text stands, a precise incident lay behind Jesus' dispute with the Pharisees and scribes (Mk 7:1-23): they had observed that the disciples of Jesus did not practise the ritual washing of hands before meals. In their eyes this constituted a transgression of the "tradition of the elders" – the *halakah*, the oral law. These Pharisaic traditions claimed to interpret and complete the Mosaic law and were considered equally authoritative and binding. Later rabbis would claim that "the ancestral laws" constituted a second, oral, law given, together with the written law, to Moses on Sinai. In responding to the charge of neglecting one observance (v 5) Jesus turned the debate on to a wider issue: the relative worth of oral law and Mosaic law. He cited Is 29:13 (in its Greek form!) against the Pharisees, drawing a parallel between "human precepts" of which Isaiah spoke and the "human tradition" on which the Pharisees counted. Jesus rejected the oral law because it was work of men (not word of God) and because it could and did conflict with the law of God. The oral law had put casuistry above love. He instanced (vv 9-13) a glaring example of casuistry run wild: a precise vow of dedication. A man might declare Korban – that is, dedicated to God – the property or capital which, by right, should go to the support of his parents. Property thus made over by vow took on a sacred character; the parents had no more claim on it. In point of fact, such a vow was legal fiction, a mean way of avoiding filial responsibility. But it was a vow and, as such, in rabbinical eyes, was binding and could not be dispensed. In this manner, a solemn duty, enjoined by Torah, was set aside. Jesus could multiply examples, he declared (v 13). He was aware that one whose mind runs to casuistry loses all sense of proportion. Minute detail becomes more and more important. Law and observance become an obsession. People are defined in terms of conformity or of "sinful" departure from it. It is a disease far worse than miserliness. For the most part, the miser nurses his own misery. Casuists are regularly in positions of authority and make life miserable for others – especially the vulnerable.

The principle of clean and unclean (a strictly ritual principle) was at the root of Jewish concern with ritual purity. A saying of Jesus (authentic in the light of the criterion of discontinuity – it is out of step with the currently accepted view) struck at the very distinction of clean and unclean, of sacred and secular: "There is nothing outside a person that by going in can defile, but the things that come out are what defile" (v 15). At one stroke Jesus had set aside the whole concept of ritual impurity. Holiness does not lie in the sphere of "clean" over against "unclean"; it is not in the realm of things but in the realm of conduct. It is to be found in the human heart and is a matter of human responsibility. Mark's parenthetical comment – "Thus he declared all foods clean" (v 19) – correctly caught the nuance of the saying. It is, more generally, a flat denial that any external things or circumstances can separate one from God (see Rom 8:38-39). We can be separated from God only through our own attitude and behaviour. In a Gentile-Christian setting this saying of v 15 was provided with a commentary (vv 17-22). The first half – nothing outside a person can defile – is explained in vv 18b-19 and the second part of the verse – it is what comes out of a person that makes one unclean – is developed in vv 20-23. In this manner it was made clear to Gentile Christians that being followers of Christ did not involve them in observance of Jewish practices. "The Way" (see Acts 9:2; 19:9, 23) is truly open to all men and women.

Jesus' contrast between word of God and human law, and his emphatic assertion of the priority of the former, are obviously of abiding validity and moment. In our day we face a particularly painful instance of a clash of interests. The eucharist is surely central to Christianity. The Christian people of God have a God-given right to the eucharist. Increasingly, the Christian people are being deprived of the eucharist on foot of a man-made regulation: mandatory celibacy. Ideology takes precedence over theology and pastoral concern. What, now, of the challenge of Jesus: "You abandon the commandment of God and hold to human tradition" (7:8)?

Divorce (10:2-12)

New Testament teaching on divorce has come under special scrutiny and Mark 10:2-12 figures prominently in all studies of the subject. In rabbinical style, question (v 2) is matched by counter-question (v 3). Nowhere in the written Torah is there legislation for divorce as such. The precise provision of Dt 24:1-4 shows divorce to be a custom taken for granted, the right of a husband to repudiate his wife without her having any redress. Jesus (Mk 10:5) does not contest his Pharisee questioner's interpretation of the law. He does declare that Moses had written the "commandment" on divorce because of human *sklérocardia*, "hardness of heart", our unteachableness, our failure to acknowledge God's moral demands and to obey the higher principle proposed in Genesis. Jesus pressed the argument further by asserting that, from the beginning, God had no divorce in mind. By creating male and female God intended marriage to be for one man and woman bound together in the indissoluble union implied by "one flesh" (Gen 1:27; 2:24). This monogamous union, moreover, was indeed unbreakable not only by reason of the two being one, but also because God brings the partners together and is author of the marriage union: "Therefore what God has joined together, let no man (i.e. husband) separate" (v 9).

An appendix (vv 10-12) to the pronouncement story is presented as an exposition which Jesus gave his disciples in private – the Marcan device which serves to adapt and broaden a teaching of Jesus. Verse 11 declares that not only is divorce forbidden but also that marriage following divorce constitutes adultery because the first marriage bond had not been severed. The words "against her", referring to a man's first wife, go beyond Jewish law which does not consider that a man commit adultery against his own wife (adultery was infringement of the right, the property indeed, of a husband). The statement in v 12 goes quite beyond Jewish law where a woman was not permitted to divorce her husband. Mark has expanded the teaching of Jesus to meet the situation of Gentile Christians living under Graeco-Roman law.

It is essential to recognize that Jesus made his pronouncement on divorce on the assumption that the marriage was a true marriage. Not only had he stressed the interpersonal relationship of husband and wife, he had, by his prohibition of divorce, struck a blow for the equality of women. Furthermore, in any treatment of the New Testament position on divorce, one must give due weight to Paul's stance in 1 Cor 7:10-16. He was fully aware of Jesus' teaching: "To the married I give this command – not I but the Lord – that the wife should not be separated from her husband" (v 10). Nevertheless, he could still advocate divorce: "if the unbelieving partner separates, let it be so; in such a case the brother or sister is not bound" (v 15). The case at issue is the marriage of a Christian and a pagan where the non-Christian spouse does not want the marriage to continue. The significant factor is that Paul, obviously, did not regard the prohibition of divorce as inflexible divine law. This is just how the Latin church has come to regard it. But, is this really what Jesus had meant? Rightly understood, his shift from what Moses wrote (Mark 10:3-4) to what God had intended (vv 6-7) – a shift from divorce to marriage – lifted the discussion out of the realm of legalism and set it in the realm of gift and grace.

The question surely must be asked whether the perception of divorce exclusively in terms of law may not account for a messy pastoral situation that cannot really be squared with the attitude and praxis of Jesus. Why is it that only in the situation of marital failure does the church seem unable to offer compassionate and effective help and healing – as it is quite able to do in all other forms of human failure and sin? Pastoral practice would be different if it were seen that Jesus proposed an ideal, one to be urged and courageously supported, but which did not paint us into a corner. And, to be honest, pastoral practice does, often enough, depart from the official line. It does when a pastor dares to ask the question: What would Jesus do?

God and Caesar (12:13-17)

This is the finest example of pronouncement story in the gospel – a story which climaxes in a notable saying of Jesus. Everything is subordinated to the pronouncement. In Mark's setting this story continues a series of controversies (11:27-12:34). As in 3:6, hostile Pharisees and Herodians came "to trap him in what he said" (12:13). Their flattery (v 14) – Jesus was an upright teacher who, without pandering to popular opinion or showing partiality, taught steadfastly the way of God – underlined their malicious intent. Ironically, their description of his character and his mission was wholly true. Their trick question bore on the mutual rights of God and of Caesar. The issue was the payment by Jews of a poll tax imposed by Rome. Generally bitterly resented, it was tolerated by Pharisees and, presumably, by Herodians (supporters of Herod

Agrippa) since both groups were prepared to go along with the status quo. A positive answer by Jesus would be offensive to nationalists; a negative answer would leave him open to being delated to the Romans since non-payment of taxes was tantamount to rebellion. The tax had to be paid in the silver coinage of Tiberius (A.D. 14-37), a coinage bearing the image of the emperor and the inscription: Tiberius Caesar, son of the divine Augustus. Jesus' request that a coin be produced, and his question, laid the basis of his answer. The validity of one's coinage was coterminous with the range of one's sovereignty. By using the coinage of Caesar, Jews were, *de facto*, acknowledging Caesar's authority and were under obligation to pay taxes to him.

Jesus' answer implies that there need not be conflict between the demands of the state and those of God. It must be remembered, however, that he held that the claims of God were all-embracing (see 12:29-30). Therefore, obligations due to the state fell within the divine order. Jesus disassociated himself from an extreme apocalyptic view (as later expressed in Revelation) which saw the Roman state as wholly evil. Christians would deduce from Jesus' principle that Christianity could accomodate loyalty to the state. But principle it remained and they had to work out the implications of it. It is not easy always to draw a clear line between a civil sphere where Caesar has his rights and a religious sphere where God rules – if such a distinction makes sense at all. It is not always easy to discern what rightfully belongs to Caesar and where loyalty to the state imposes unacceptable demands. Mark's readers, at least, would have learned from bitter experience that rendering to God the things that are God's had brought them into conflict with the state (13:8-11). Jesus taught no neat doctrine of the relationship of church and state. The church must continue, in changing and fluctuating social and cultural conditions, to sort out its obligations, to discern as honestly as possible what is due to God and what to Caesar. What history shows, unequivocally, is that separation of church and state is absolutely essential.

Riches (10:17-31)

Jesus' teaching on the danger of riches (10:23-27) and on the reward of renunciation (10:28-31) was provoked by the incident of 10:17-32.

This is the saddest story in the gospel, this story (vv 17-22) of the refusal of one whom Jesus loved to answer his call. Entry into the kingdom is the matter and issue as Jesus was asked what one must do to inherit eternal life. He began to answer the question by pointing to the duties towards one's neighbour prescribed in the decalogue; but he knew that observance of the law was not the whole answer. He was drawn to the man and invited him to become his disciple. This aspiring disciple had to learn that discipleship is costly: he, a wealthy man, was asked to surrender the former basis of his security and find his security in Jesus' word. He failed to see that following Jesus was the true treasure, the one pearl of great price (Mt 13:44, 46) beyond all his possessions. He could not face the stern challenge of loving in deed and in truth by opening his heart to his brother or sister in need (see 1 Jn 3:17-18).

The rich man's sad departure (Mk 10:22) was dramatic evidence that riches could come between a person and the following of Jesus; the words of Jesus (vv 23-27) drove the message home. Jesus began by stressing the difficulty, for the wealthy, of access to the kingdom (v 33) and passed quickly to the difficulty of entering the kingdom at all (v 24). A vivid example of the impossible – "It is easier for a camel to go through the eye of a needle than for someone who is rich to enter the kingdom of God" (v 25) (contrast of the largest beast known in Palestine with the smallest domestic aperture) – applied as it is to the rich would come more logically before v 24. The point is that salvation is ever God's achievement, never that of humans (v 27). It is the only answer, the confident answer, to the helpless question, "Then who can be saved?" (v 26). Seemingly complex, a paraphrase of 10:23-26 shows that the thought is not difficult to follow: How hard indeed it is for anyone to enter the kingdom, but for rich people it is quite impossible. In fact, humanly speaking, it is impossible for anyone to be saved, rich or not; but with God all things are possible. This is Paul's teaching in Romans.

All attempts to soften the hard saying of Jesus (v 25) contradict Mark's obvious intent. The concern throughout vv 17-31 was the problem of wealth in relation to the kingdom of God. The fact that the disciples were reported as being "perplexed" (v 24) and "astounded" (v 26) at Jesus' words, together with their question with regard to who can be saved (v 26), suggests that they believed the prosperity of the rich to be a sign of God's blessing. Mark, however, has presented wealth as a stumbling block or insurmountable barrier on the way to the kingdom. Can the rich be saved?

In the verses under discussion (10:23-27) Jesus pointed out that salvation for the rich was possible, but it was possible only through the power of God (v 27). The point of this saying is that God will have to work a miracle of conversion in the hearts of the rich in order for them to be saved. It is so hard for those with wealth to divest themselves of their material possessions, and the security and power that seem to come with them, that it will take divine intervention to free the rich from their bondage.

The verses which follow (10:28-31) direct the reader's attention to a group of individuals, Peter and the disciples, who have overcome the temptation of possessions and left their families, homes and occupations to follow Jesus in a life of discipleship. This does not mean, however, that to be a disciple one must be destitute. Jesus promised that those who forsake all for the kingdom will receive a hundredfold in this life. Despite his pattern as itinerant prophet and teacher, Jesus was no ascetic. The life of the poor, with its hardship and suffering, is not set forth in Mark's gospel as an ideal for the Christian disciple. But, neither is the desire for possessions nor the accumulation of wealth a reflection of the will of God.

The disciples had left all; Peter stated the fact with some complacency (10:28). His implicit question is made explicit in Mt 19:27 – "What then will we have?" The items listed (v 29), given disjunctively, included all possessions under the heads of home, relatives and property. Significant is an omission in v 30. Verse 29 runs: "No one who has left house or brothers or sisters or mother or father or children or fields," while v 30 runs: "houses, brothers and sisters, mothers and children, and fields" – "fathers" are absent! This is a factor in the growing evidence that Jesus had envisaged a discipleship of equals. He surely did not have in mind (given his distinctive view of authority) a patriarchal model of authority, with its pattern of domination.

Scribes and widow (12:38-44)
The scribes of the gospels were interpreters of Old Testament law –

in our terms, theologians and lawyers. They prided themselves on their expertize and – many of them being Pharisees – on their meticulous religious observance. On both scores they (or some among them) invited and received deference; to that end they affected distinctive dress. It ought surely be of more than academic interest that the Jesus-tradition is critical of "churchly" dress and "ecclesiastical" lifestyle. The scribes claimed the "best seats" in the synagogue: directly in front of the ark containing the sacred scrolls and facing the people. The charge in v 40 is more serious: "They devour widows' houses and for the sake of appearance say long prayers." Judaism had some scathing condemnations of unscrupulous scribes. The sweeping tone of the charges here, however, reflects the animosity between the church and official Judaism, an animosity more trenchantly expressed in Matthew 23.

This portrait of the scribes stands, and was meant to stand in sharp contrast to the attitude and conduct of Christian leaders (9:33-37; 10:42-45). What has been, and continues to be, the reality in the church? Distinctive dress, honorific titles, signs of deference, places of honour at religious and civic functions! It is not easy to see a difference between such practice and the conduct of the scribes outlined and censured here in vv 38-39.

The widow's mite (12:41-44)

This vignette may have found its setting here partly because of the catchword "widow" (vv 40,42). More importantly, it is in place because, as an example of genuine Jewish piety, it contrasts with the counterfeit piety of the scribes (or, of scribes characterized in vv 38-39). The poor widow who received Jesus' approbation represents the common people. The "copper coin" (*lepton*) was the smallest in circulation. Mention of two coins is important: the woman might have kept one for herself. Wealthy people had been generous (v 41). This poor widow's mite was an immeasurably greater gift than theirs, for she had given of her all – her "whole living" (v 44). She had let go of every shred of security and had committed herself wholly to God.

Such is the traditional interpretation of the passage. But we may, and most likely should, view it in a different light. Would Jesus really have approved of, and lauded, a poor widow giving "out of her poverty... all that she had to live on"? Hardly. His directly pre-ceding castigation of the scribes as those who "devour widows' houses" is (at least in Mark's arrangement) surely in mind. This poor widow was a victim of religious establishment. She had been convinced that it was a "holy" thing to give her all to the Temple.[12] She is a tragic example of a situation Jesus had in mind when he declared: "Religion is for men and women, not men and women for religion."

Resurrection (12:18-27)

The Sadducees were a priestly and aristocratic party whose theology was traditionalist and conservative. They were not prepared to accept the newfangled doctrine of resurrection (see Acts 23:8). The pronouncement story of Mk 12:18-27 enshrines their objection to it and Jesus' reply. The case they presented – designed to show that belief in resurrection leads to absurdity – is based on the law of levi-rate marriage (Dt 25:5-10). The law was in abeyance but could be invoked in theological argument. Jesus' rejoinder was that the Sadducees had not understood the power of God who is capable of achieving something beyond human imagining and, in particular, of making resurrection-life notably different from life on earth. That is the point of the punch-line: "For when they rise from the dead, they neither marry nor are given in marriage, but are like angels in heaven" (12:25). The statement presents a more sophisticated, as opposed to a popular, notion of resurrection: it will effect a radical transformation.

In vv 26-27 Jesus turned to the fact of resurrection. In Exodus 3:6 Yahweh declared: "I am ... the God of Abraham, the God of Isaac and the God of Jacob." By the time of Moses the three patriarchs had long been dead. And yet, because their God is always God of the living, the patriarchs must, though dead, have been destined for life; they will be raised to life. He had named himself their God, he had made promises to them which could not fail (see Rom 11:29), promises which death could not annul. Their hope of resurrection lay in fellowship with God. By standards of modern exegesis this rabbinical-style argument is hardly convincing. Yet, the reason for life beyond death adduced here is congenial to modern men and women. "Proofs" based on the immortality of the soul, presupposing a questionable dichotomy between "soul" and "body", are not helpful. For the Christian the real ground of immortality is fellowship with the risen Lord and with the living God. Paul has said it all: "thanks be to God who gives us the victory (over death) through our Lord Jesus Christ" (1 Cor 15:57).

CONCLUSION

In Jesus the roles of prophet and teacher overlapped – as they did, regularly, in the prophets of Israel. Jesus taught distinctively. And he taught with authority. As a first-century Palestinian Jew he, of course, shared much of the theology of his tradition. But there was more than enough to set him apart. The ultimate factor was his understanding of God. Clashes with his relingous opponents over matters of law, such as sabbath observance, were symptomatic of fundamental difference. Jesus knew, better than any other, that to proclaim one's belief in God is not enough. What matters, and matters utterly, is the kind of God in whom one believes. It makes, literally, a world of difference whether one's God is the true God or a distorted image of that God. For Jesus, God is God of humankind. He is found where there is goodness and a striving for the liberation of humankind. We are human beings, created in the image of God; we are meant to image God. Our destiny is to be human – as God understands humanness. The corollary is that only with God can we reach full humanness. Jesus, with God, reached whole humanness.

Here, it is widely believed, is where religion comes in. Religion, generally seen as the area of humankind's relation with God, is ostensibly a system and manner of life that unites us with God, that enables us to be godly. Like all things human, religion is subject to corruption. The temptation of the relingous person is to identify one's man-made world with the world of God and claim control over the holy. In practice, religion may be a barrier to creative union with God; it may lock us into a narrow, impoverished way. Jesus uttered his word, at once criterion and critique: "The sabbath was made for humankind, and not humankind for the sabbath" (Mk 2:27). Decoded, it runs: "Religion is in the service of men and women; men and women are not slaves of religion." Wherever religion is burden, wherever it shows lack of respect for human freedom, it has become oppressor, not servant.[13] Authentic religion must foster freedom. Of course, one has to understand freedom correctly. In a Christian context, freedom is never licence to do as one pleases. Paradoxically, the ultimate freedom is freedom to serve. "The Son of Man came not to be served but to serve, and to give his life as a ransom for many" (10:45). Here is the sure christological basis of authentic freedom.

Mark has presented Jesus as Teacher and he gave an indication of the range of his teaching. One thing emerges, unmistakably: Jesus had an eschatological perspective indeed – but he was deeply concerned with life in the here and now. He sought to reform Israel: he desired the fabric of life in his day to be transformed. Jesus had a refreshingly realistic understanding of salvation. Salvation happens in our world, in our history. Salvation comes from God but happens, as it must, in the lives of human beings. It reaches into and touches every aspect of human life. Otherwise it would not be salvation of humankind. Salvation is not confined within the limits of religion. Indeed, too often, religion is and has been an obstacle to salvation – the whole liberation of the wholly human. And it is only where men and women are free to be truly human that the human person becomes the image of God. It is only so that the true being of God may be revealed. Being image of God is not only the reflection of God but the revelation of God. Jesus of Nazareth, in Mark's portrait, is supremely the image of God. The Marcan Jesus is, transparently, the one "like his brothers and sisters in every respect" who is, at the same time, and in his sheer humanness, "the reflection of God's glory and the exact imprint of God's very being" (Heb 2:17; 1:3).

Demanding teacher

Jesus offers no soft option. Christians may be children of God but only on condition that they understand what this means and live what it demands. The manner of being child of God has been firmly traced: "Anyone who wants to be a follower of mine must renounce self, take up one's cross and follow me" (Mk 8:34). Jesus delivered a challenge, the challenge of his own way as Son. Being a disciple is a serious business. Yet, taking up one's cross is not at all to say that suffering is something Christians should seek. Jesus did not seek suffering; Gethsemane is clear enough. But, suffering will be part of Christian life as it was part of Jesus' life. The comfort is that the fol-

lowing can be in tiny steps. God is patient. His challenge is invitation. Faithfulness to one's way of life, concern for others in whatever manner, the caring gesture, the kind word – these add up. There
will be heroes, the few; there will be those whose way will seem
ordinary, drab – the many. Even in the things of God we are prone
to measure by worldly standards. The Lord does not overlook the
painful decision, the unspoken sorrow, the secret suffering. There
are many more saints than those whom we honour as such. It
would be wise not to overlook the minor characters of Mark's
gospel.

It shall not be so

In the religious sphere, Jesus could not avoid a clash with the religious authorities of Judaism. He did not set out to challenge, head-
on, social and political structures. One should note, however, that
his paradoxical view of authority was subversive of authority as
domination. One might go further and maintain that while his
attack on "unclean spirits" was, in fact, an attack on disease, his war
against "Satan" was war against oppressive and dehumanizing
power structures. Jesus always aimed at root causes. It is not surprising, then, that there is no evidence of his ever having taken a
specific stand against Roman domination. For that matter, when
challenged, he declared: "Give to the emperor the things that are
the emperor's, and to God the things that are God's" (12:17). The
tenor of his teaching made clear his assumption that Caesar's claim
would be just: he did not grant Caesar a blank cheque. His concern
went far deeper than any given political entity. And never would
he envisage violence as a way to political and social change. His
demand, "Love your enemy," is a radical disavowal of violence. It
is a challenge which carries within it the seed of the destruction of
violence.

The authority of Jesus

It is clear from the gospels that Jesus had *exousia* – authority – from
God. It is equally clear that this power of his did not have any shade
of domination. Mark does indeed show Jesus having facile authority
over evil spirits – the exorcisms, and over nature – the stilling of the
tempest. But Jesus' authority did not extend to lording it over people.
For that matter, in relation to people, he was largely helpless. The

hallmark of the use of his authority in relation to people was consistently and emphatically that of *diakonia*, service. If Jesus did serve others, it was always from a position of strength. He would not do what others wanted him to do unless it be consonant with God's will. He would lead, but he would not control. He healed, both physically and spiritually, looking for nothing else than openness to his healing touch. He was friend of sinners – and we must not allow ourselves subconsciously to think that they were repentant sinners before he was their friend. No, he befriended them in their brokenness.

Jesus certainly confronted the religious authorities, but without seeking to impose his authority on them. He was content to hold the mirror up to them, urging them to discern in their attitude and conduct a betrayal of God's rule. But that was the measure of it. Response was their responsibility. Jesus sought no advantage from his authority. He laid claim to no titles – it was up to others to identify him. In his healing ministry Jesus became the man who relieved suffering. At the end he was the vulnerable one who became victim of suffering. He was, after all, the one who had come "to serve, and to give his life as a ransom for many" (Mk 10:45). In short, Jesus, in his authority as in all else, mirrored God. For God, the God of infinite power, is never a God of force. The Son never did, nor ever would, resort to force.

CHAPTER 5

Healer

Those who are well have no need of a physician, but those who are sick;
I have come to call not the righteous but sinners. (Mk 2:17).

Miracles

All four gospels agree that Jesus worked miracles – and not just a
few but many. Miracle has been aptly defined by John Meier:

> A miracle is (1) an unusual, startling, or extraordinary event that
> is in principle perceivable by any interested and fair-minded
> observer, (2) an event which finds no reasonable explanation in
> human abilities or in other known forces that operate in our
> world of time and space, and (3) an event that is the result of a
> special act of God, doing what no human power can do.[14]

Recognition of miracle as such is always a philosophical or theological judgment. It is not possible for historian or exegete, in terms of
their disciplines, to judge that God has acted in this or that event in
a manner beyond human power. With regard to the gospel miracles
a number of questions need to be asked. Are reports of miracles
attributed to Jesus creations of the early church, or can some at least
of these reports be traced back to the time and activity of the historical Jesus? Did Jesus, in fact, perform actions acknowledged as miracles by himself and his followers? If so, what did these miracles
mean in the context of his ministry?

In the modern world, many find it difficult to accomodate the
notion of miracle; many reject the possibility of miracle. In contrast,
in the Graeco-Roman world of Jesus' day, miracles were quite will-
ingly acknowledged. If Jesus did perform miracles they would
readily be accepted as such by his contemporaries. The question is:
did he, in fact, perform miracles? Here the familiar criteria of multiple

attestation and coherence come into play.[15] The criterion of multiple attestation is here twofold: multiple sources – all four gospels carry accounts of several miracles; multiple literary forms – exorcism stories, healing stories and accounts of nature miracles. The criterion of coherence discerns an impressive convergence of actions and sayings of Jesus; miracle stories do fit into the pattern of his deeds and words. These criteria firmly support the tradition of Jesus' miracles. It is reasonably certain that Jesus did perform startling deeds regarded by himself and others as miracles. Among these were, assuredly, deeds of healing.

HEALINGS

Jesus' reputation as healer is emphatically attested by all four evangelists. This healing activity covered a range of afflictions: paralysis, blindness, leprosy, deafness and other ailments. Mark has instances across the board. Because our purpose is to discern and manifest the Marcan Jesus, we will look at these healings not by category but in the sequence of the gospel of Mark.

Peter's mother-in-law (Mk 1:29-31)

"A day in the life of Jesus" (Mk 1:21-34) illustrates a feature of the early ministry: the authority of Jesus in terms of teaching and exorcism and healing. In healing Peter's mother-in-law (1:29-31) Jesus, who had performed an exorcism (1:23-26), is shown to have power over sickness. Like the exorcisms, the miracles of healing, too, were signs of salvation. The early Christian community was not interested in the miracles of Jesus as brute facts. It regarded them in a twofold light: as a manifestation of the power of God active in Jesus and as signs of the redemption which Jesus had wrought. In the present healing story the phrase he "lifted her up" (*egeiró*, "to lift up" also means "raise from the dead") has symbolic meaning. The woman "lifted" from "fever" symbolized one formerly prostrate beneath the thrall of sin and now raised up by the Lord and called upon to to serve him.

At the close of this specimen day, "all" the sick and possessed of the town were brought to Jesus (vv 32-34). This summarizing passage (such summaries are typical of Mark) describes Jesus' mission up to now and marks a transition to the further spread of his activity. The demons (v 34) understood, as the crowds and the disciples did not, that Jesus was the envoy of God, and were bound to silence. The "secret" – the imposition of silence, by Jesus, throughout the gospel – has to do with the true status of Jesus. Mark is sure that what "Son of God" means can be understood only when Jesus had shown, through suffering and death, what it means. That is why Jesus cannot be acclaimed "until after the Son of Man had risen from the dead" (9:9).

You can make me clean (1:40-45)

The passage 1:40-45 sits lightly in its Marcan context. We may discern, in the current attitude towards leprosy, a reason for the evangelist's insertion of it at this point. Leprosy (a term which in the Bible covers a variety of skin diseases, see Leviticus 13) was regarded as the ultimate uncleanness which cut the afflicted one off from the community as being a source of ritual defilement for others. Significantly, in the New Testament, the removal of leprosy is not described as healing but as "cleansing". The law was helpless in regard to leprosy; it could only defend the community against the leper. But what the law could not achieve, Jesus accomplished.

According to the more widely attested reading, Jesus was moved with "pity" at the petition of the wretched man (v 41). There can be little doubt that "moved with anger", not nearly so well attested, is the original reading. It is easy to understand why copyists would have changed it to "moved with pity"; it is incredible that they should have done the reverse. The anger of Jesus was twofold. It was his reaction to a disease which brought him face to face with the ravages of evil – all disease, it was thought, was caused by evil forces. More deeply it was because the unfortunate man had been branded a pariah. His disease had cut him off from social and religious life. Child of God, he was not permitted to come into the presence of God. If one were to touch him – even his garment – one became "unclean", unworthy to approach God. Thus can religion distort the graciousness of God. Jesus stepped forward, reached out and firmly laid his hand on the man – no concern with uncleanness there! He was healed. The law (Lev 14:2-32) specified that one who claimed to be healed of leprosy should have the cure verified by a priest. In bidding the man to carry out the prescription, Jesus intended something more. "As a testimony to them" (v 44) is to be taken as a challenge to the priesthood and their view of things – it is testimony against them (see 6:11). Jesus was already aware that the priests did not look kindly upon his ministry. Who are the "lepers", the outcasts, of our day? One readily thinks of, among others, those suffering from AIDS. Does one need to ask how Jesus would treat them? He would surely be "moved with anger" at how unkindly they are categorized by some "Christians."

To save life or to kill (3:1-6)

Jesus had been carrying out his mission in Galilee: teaching, healing, exorcizing. Soon comes confrontation – with various opponents. It is documented in a series of five controversies (2:1-3:6). The passage 2:1-12 is the first of the conflict stories. The passage is composite, with vv 1-5a, 11-12 forming a coherent miracle story. Through insertion of a section on the remission of sins (vv 5b-10), Mark has turned the narrative into a controversy story. The healing narrative proper gives a striking instance of the faith needful for the reception of a miracle (see 6:5-6). Noteworthy is the specifying here of vicarious faith – "when Jesus saw their faith" (v 5), that of the enterprising four who had determinedly dug through a roof to get their paralysed friend into the presence of Jesus. See 7:25-30; 9:24.

The fifth conflict story (3:1-6) is the climax of the series. Here Jesus himself is more aggressive and the plot against him (v 6) points to the inevitable end of the persistent hostility. But the issue was, too, of immediate interest to Mark's community. If Christians had chosen to observe the Lord's day (Sunday) rather than the Jewish sabbath, they had, nonetheless, opted for a form of sabbath observance. The question was: how far to push that observance and in what spirit. The challenge to Jesus and his deed of mercy (v 4) will have given them their principle and their pattern.

A trap had been set for Jesus: a man with a withered hand was positioned prominently in the synagogue. Jesus was angry. They were callously using this poor man as bait. One does not treat people so. They were making a mockery of the sabbath. He healed the man; the Pharisees promptly accused Jesus of an infringement of sabbath observance. He viewed the matter in a wholly different light and

challenged their attitude. In forbidding healing on the sabbath the
rabbis would equivalently admit that, on this day, moral values
were reversed: it was forbidden to "do good" and prescribed to "do
evil". (Note the querulous synagogue leader of Luke 13:14 in reaction to Jesus' healing of a crippled woman on a sabbath: "There are
six days on which work ought to be done; come on those days to be
cured, and not on the sabbath day.") The real issue is no longer
what one is permitted to do; it is the obligation of doing good at all
times and in all circumstances. Jesus asked: "Is it lawful to do good
or to do harm on the sabbath, to save life or to kill?" How sad that
the spirit of legalism has so regularly and so firmly asserted itself in
the Christian church. We have been so eager to multiply rules and
to impose them, so anxious to measure our Christianity by the
punctiliousness of our "observance."

Your faith has saved you (5:21-43)

The dovetailing of one story with another – his "sandwich" technique – is a feature of Mark's style. Nowhere else does an insertion
so clearly separate two parts of a story as it does in 5:21-43. (21-24a,
[24b-34], 35-43). Each "sandwich" of Mark is a carefully constructed
unit and should be read as such. Salvation and faith are the major
themes of our twin narrative. Jairus was confident that at Jesus'
touch his daughter would be "made well" (v 23) and the woman is
persuaded that if she were to touch Jesus' garments she would be
"made well" (v 28). Each time the verb is *sózó* which means also "to
save." More pointedly, in v 34, Jesus reassured the woman, telling
her, "Your faith has made you well – has saved you." Mark had in
mind more than bodily healing. Salvation stands in close relationship to faith. Jesus, then, exhorted the father of the dead girl, "Do
not fear, only believe" (v 36).

Furthermore, the evangelist lets it be understood that the narrative
of the daughter of Jairus is a manifestation of the power of the risen
Lord. Jesus said to the girl, "'Little girl, get up! (arise)'. And immediately the little girl got up (arose)." The verbs "to arise" *(egeirein)*
and "to rise up" *(anistémi)* are used of the resurrection of Jesus
(14:28; 16:6 and 8:31; 9:9-10; 10:34). Confirmation of the theological
importance of the raising accomplished by Jesus is the exclusive
presence of the three privileged witnesses, Peter, James and John

(5:37) who were also alone with Jesus at the transfiguration (9:2), in Gethsemane (14:3) and (with Andrew) on the Mount of Olives as hearers of the farewell discourse (13:3). Each time their presence is a pointer to the reader: here is something especially significant. Jesus raises the dead girl to life because he is "the resurrection and the life" (Jn 11:25). For Mark and his readers he is the Lord, source of saving power (5:30) and the narrative is a lesson in salvation through faith.

Faith comes to fulfilment in personal encounter with Jesus, in dialogue with him. Jairus believed that Jesus had power to heal one on the point of death (5:23). Jesus looked for a deeper faith: faith in him as one who could raise from the dead, a faith finding expression in the midst of unbelief (5:35-36). The woman, too, had faith in the power of Jesus (5:27-28). She, too, was asked to have a fuller faith in him; she met his gaze and came to kneel at his feet (5:33). And, through faith in Jesus, she and the little girl were made well – saved. The Christian is asked to recognize that faith in Jesus can transform life and is victory over death. This faith is not something vague or impersonal. One must kneel at his feet, not abjectly, but in the intensity of one's pleading (v 22) or in humble thankfulness (v 33). This Jesus will give to one who believes that peace the world cannot give (v 34). He will assure that person of life beyond death (v 41).

The Woman

This encounter with a troubled woman gives us a precious glimpse of the courtesy of Jesus. On the way to Jairus' home he had sensed that a person of faith had invoked his healing power, by touching his cloak. He asked, "Who touched my clothes?" (5:30). His blunt disciples looked at him, pityingly: he was thronged by a crowd and complained that someone had touched him! (v 31). Jesus knew who that someone was: a woman. A woman, moreover, who suffered from a chronic haemorrhage and was, therefore, ritually unclean. She had no business being in a crowd and, by touching Jesus, had rendered him ritually unclean also; or, so others would have reckoned. While, for her, the social consequences were not as grave as for the unfortunate leper (1:40-41), she was obliged to live in quiet isolation. Jesus had no patience with such restrictive purity regulations. He was concerned with people, intent on liberation from physical and social suffering. Jesus did not scold the woman for her "reprehensible" conduct. Instead, he commended her faith. And he made a point, not only of speaking gently to her, but of addressing her, respectfully, as "Daughter", that is, daughter of Abraham and Sarah, a child of God.

Raising the Dead

To our way of thinking, raising the dead is simply not on; there really is no place for it in our culture. In contrast, many of Jesus' day would have regarded the matter more sympathetically and have been prepared to accept that a holy man might raise the dead to life. For Jews there were the parallel stories of Elijah (1 Kgs 17:17-24) and Elisha (2 Kgs 4:18-37). As for the gospels, the criterion of multiple attestation is a factor: Mk 5:21-43, parr., the special Lucan tradition (Lk 7:11-17), Jn 11:1-46 – the raising, respectively, of the daughter of Jairus, son of the widow of Nain, and Lazarus. Despite this spread, the basic question is: are these stories creations of the early church, or may they spring from events in the life of Jesus? It surely is not without significance that the other evangelists show no awareness of the Nain (Luke) and Lazarus (John) stories.

Our concern is the raising of the daughter of Jairus. Whatever did occur, it looks as though Mark regarded it as a raising from the dead. Still, there is that observation of Jesus: "The child is not dead but sleeping" (v 41). This might indicate his more perceptive diagnosis: the child was in a coma, not dead as others thought (see 9:26). A number of factors combine to suggest that the Jairus story ultimately goes back to an incident in the life of the historical Jesus. At the close of a thorough study, John Meier's conclusion is:

> The convergence of all the considerations in one miracle story – its lengthy tradition history, the unusual mentioning of the petitioner's name and his status as a synagogue ruler, the indications of a Semitic substratum and especially the striking *talitha koum*, the absence of any christological title or affirmation, and the elements of embarrasment and discontinuity – incline me to the view that the Jairus story does reflect and stem from some event in Jesus' public ministry. In other words, the story is not an invention of the early church pure and simple, however much it may have been expanded and reinterpreted by Christian faith.[16]

The story might well be seen as dramatisation of the life-giving power of Jesus.

He has done all things well (7:31-37)

Mark has set the healing of a deaf-mute (7:31-37) in the Gentile region of Decapolis (east of the Jordan); as in his previous episode (the exorcism of a Gentile woman's daughter [7:24-30]), he is concerned with Jesus' attitude to the Gentiles. In that story, the casting out of the unclean spirit which possessed the Gentile girl showed Jesus hearkening to Gentiles and setting them free. This time, in a Gentile setting, a man recovers his faculty of hearing and speaking. The healing has the symbolic intent of showing that the Gentiles, once deaf and dumb towards God, are now capable of hearing God and rendering him homage. They, too, have become heirs of the eschatological promise to Israel: "The ears of the deaf will be unstopped ... and the tongue of the speechless sing for joy" (Is 35:5-6).

Jesus' action of putting his fingers into the man's ears and of touching his tongue with spittle, were common to the techniques of Greek and Jewish healers. Here the gestures have a certain "sacramental" quality (see 8:23). "Looking up to heaven," as in 6:41, implies Jesus' intimacy with God. "Sigh" expresses his deep sympathy with the sufferer (see 1:41). "Be opened" – characteristically, Mark translated the Aramaic word *ephphatha*. The description of this cure (v 35) is given solemn cast (the parallel cure in chapter 8 will be described, too, in three clauses [8:25]). Disobedience of the stereotyped injunction to preserve silence is put very strongly: "Jesus ordered them to tell no one; but the more he ordered them, the more zealously they proclaimed it" (v 36). As in 1:45 the deed was "proclaimed": the deeds of Jesus cannot but speak the good news. Astonishment was "beyond measure," the strongest statement of astonishment in Mark; the miracle has exceptional significance. "He has done everything well" recalls Gen 1:31. We may also discern in the Greek chorus of the crowd (v 37) the response in faith of the Christian community who perceived in the works of Jesus the time of fulfilment announced by Isaiah.

The cure of a blind man (8:22-26)

The situation of the story of the healing of a blind man (8:22-26) is calculated and its symbolic intent is manifest. It comes, dramatically, just after the castigation of the sheer hardness of heart, the total blindness, of the disciples (8:14-21). It thereby symbolizes the gradual opening of their eyes leading, at last, to a profession of faith (8:27-29). Indeed, the parallelism between vv 22-26 and 27-30 is remarkable. Jesus led the disciples away from the village(s), 27a (23a), and in two stages, at first imperfectly, 27b-28 (23-24), then fully, 29 (25), the truth about him was made plain. Jesus then imposed silence, 30 (26). The story is a sign of coming to faith. It tells us that Jesus alone could cure the blindness of the disciples; and it shows, too, that their lack of understanding was so serious that it could be penetrated only gradually. The second half of the gospel will show how imperfect that first glimmer of understanding was and how Jesus will have to struggle with their persistent obtuseness. The readers of the gospel are reminded that only the Lord can grant understanding.

Bethsaida was a town on the north shore of the lake, just east of the Jordan mouth. For Mark (6:45) this was "the other side". "They brought to him ... and begged him to" (v 22) – verbally the same as 7:32. Again in v 23 there is much in common with 7:33 – the taking of the man aside, the use of spittle and the laying on of hands. "Can you see anything?" – the question of Jesus in the course of working a miracle was unusual. This is the only cure in the gospels that is described as taking place gradually, in two stages. This factor may well have been a traditional device to bring out more graphically the difficulty of the healing and so add to the impressiveness of the miracle. But Mark saw it as an illustration of growth in faith (see vv 27-29). "I can see people, but they look like trees, walking" (v 24) is a good rendering of an awkward Greek sentence. The idea is clear: the man was beginning to recover his sight, but as yet could not distinguish objects clearly. As in 7:35 the cure itself is vividly described in three co-ordinated phrases (v 25). "Do not even go into the village" (v 26); another, and preferable, reading is: "Do not tell anyone in the village." This alternative reading would constitute a further link with the cure of the deaf mute: "Then he ordered them to tell no one" (7:36).

There is another healing of a blind man, Bartimaeus, at 10:46-52. These two stories (8:22-26; 10:46-52) frame the intervening section.

They stand, respectively, at the beginning and at the end of the way to Jerusalem and draw our attention to what Jesus had been doing: on the way he had striven to open the eyes of his disciples.

He followed him on the way (10:46-52)

This narrative focuses on the blind man, who is thereby presented as a model of faith in Jesus in spite of discouragement, and as one who eagerly answered the call of the Master and followed him in the way of discipleship. The story is as much a call story as a healing story. For Mark the story sounds a new departure in the self-manifestation of Jesus. He heard himself acclaimed, repeatedly, as "Son of David", a messianic title. Far from imposing silence, as hitherto, he called the man to his presence and openly restored his sight. The days were near for him to be delivered up and he had set his face to go to Jerusalem (10:32; see Lk 9:51). Very soon the true nature of his messiahship would be clearly seen.

Jesus asked the man, "What do you want me to do for you?" (10:51). The question is the same as that, just before (v 36), to the brothers James and John in response to their request: "Teacher, we want you to do for us whatever we ask of you." (v 35). The simple and humble request of Bartimaeus, "Rabbouni, let me see again" was so different from their arrogant demand; he understood so much better than they the authority of a Jesus who had come to serve (vv 42-45). Unlike them (v 39) he was aware of his need and his helplessness and found his only hope in Jesus' nearness. And Jesus' responded to his need: "Your faith has made you well" (v 52). Would the disciples learn from Bartimaeus, learn that Jesus' "authority" was wholly in the service of healing and growth? "Faith" is confident trust in God and in the healing power of Jesus (see 5:34). "Made you well" – saved you – has the same overtones of salvation as in 5:28,34. "Followed him on the way" (v 52) could mean that the man joined the crowd on their way to Jerusalem. But Jesus had opened his eyes to a deeper reality. There can be no doubt that Mark intends: he followed Jesus on the way of Christian discipleship. The phrase "on the way" and the following of Jesus form an inclusion with v 32 – "They were on the road, going up to Jerusalem, and Jesus was walking ahead of them; they were amazed, and those who followed were afraid." Only one of faith, enlightened by Jesus, one like Bartimaeus, can walk the way of Jesus without consternation and without fear.

CONCLUSION

Jesus' reputation as miracle-worker is firmly established in the gospels. The majority of the miracles are healings of varied diseases. This healing activity was not only motivated by his concern for suffering, his sympathy with the afflicted. It was also a sign of the inbreak of the kingdom. The saving power of God was making its way into the lives of men and women.

The first healing (as distinct from the exorcism of 1:21-28) recorded by Mark is the healing of a woman. We have noted the symbolic overtones; the deed, however, retains its own significance. Of quite special interest are the other healings of a woman and a little girl (5:21-43). Here, too, Jesus' courtesy (5:31) and practical concern (5:43b) were very much in evidence. Mark had built the double story into an elaborate catechesis of salvation by faith and into an anticipation of the resurrection power of the Lord.

The cleansing of a leper (1:40-45) highlights Jesus' predilection for outcasts. His anger at the situation was a facet of his impatience with a religious attitude that puts observance before people. The point was made more sharply in the synagogue incident (3:1-6). A cripple was callously used as bait: what will Jesus do? He was angered by the shameful exploitation of a human being. He was angered by a stultifying legalism that would outlaw a good deed – on the sabbath! He had, from the first, stressed that all people were to be respected. He had, before, in regard to the sabbath, insisted that the sabbath was God's gift to humankind. It had been perverted into a burden (2:27). Jesus was critical of the religious observance of his day. It is not in doubt that the Marcan Jesus would be no less scathing of much of the religious observance of today.

Two healings of the blind (8:22-26; 10:46-52) come at strategic points in the gospel. The first is related to the blindness of the disciples (8:11-21). It can be healed only gradually, and Jesus alone can bring it about. The passage 8:22-26 is introduction to the Caesarea Philippi episode where, at first sight, the disciples (Peter) do see. It is made starkly clear that they did not understand (8:27-33). Peter's confession, "You are the Messiah" (8:29) is a classic example of "verbal orthodoxy". The formula is impeccable; the understanding of it was wholly wide of the mark (8:32-33). Today there does appear to be a preoccupation with "orthodoxy". It seems to be enough to make the right noises and adopt the right stances. There does not seem to be over much concern with a flawed image of God or a docetist christology that lurk behind the words and the attitudes.

Bartimaeus (10:46-52) emerges as one of Mark's minor characters – as one of the most eloquent of them. He was a man of faith who would not be dissuaded from turning to Jesus in his need. If his initial confession of Jesus as Son of David was insufficient, though correct, Bartimaeus, unlike Peter, would not persist in his stubborness because Bartimaeus did not "set his mind on human things" (see 8:33). He came to recognize Jesus and followed him on the way of discipleship. Would the disciples learn from Bartimaeus that Jesus' "authority" was wholly in the service of healing and growth?

CHAPTER 6

Exorcist

If it is by the finger of God that I cast out demons,
then the kingdom of God has come to you. (Lk 11:20).

Prominent among Jesus' miraculous deeds – especially so in Mark – were exorcisms. This aspect of Jesus' activity can and does upset our modern sensibility. The situation is aggravated by theatrical exploitation of the subject and by quite harmful interventions of would-be "exorcists." In the world of Jesus, on the other hand, exorcism was readily accepted both in paganism and in Judaism. It is, then, to be expected rather than come as a surprise, that Jesus figured as an exorcist. John P. Meier comments:

> However disconcerting it may be to modern sensibilities, it is fairly certain that Jesus was, among other things, a first-century Jewish exorcist and probably won not a little of his fame and following by practicing exorcisms … Perhaps in no other aspect of Jesus' ministry does his distance from modern Western culture and scientific technology loom so large and the facile program of making the historical Jesus instantly relevant to present-day men and women seem so ill-conceived. One can approach his exorcisms with greater sympathy if one remembers that Jesus no doubt saw them as part of his overall ministry of healing and liberating the people of Israel from the illnesses and other physical and spiritual evils that beset them. Granted the primitive state of medical knowledge in the first-century Mediterranean world, mental illness, psychosomatic diseases, and such afflictions as epilepsy were often attributed to demonic possession. If Jesus saw himself called to battle against these evils, which diminished the lives of his fellow Israelites, it was quite natural for him, as a first-century Jew, to understand this specific dimension of his ministry in terms of exorcism. All of this simply underscores the obvious: Jesus was a man and a Jew of his times.[17]

An obvious corollary is that a twentieth-century Jesus would view the situation very differently; he would not be an exorcist. We must adjust our perspective to a first-century worldview. In our look at the Marcan exorcisms (1:23-28; 5:1-10; 7:24-30; 9:14-29) we prescind from the question whether or not all (or any) are historical. They are presented by the evangelist as deeds of Jesus, and we are concerned with the Jesus of Mark.

An unclean spirit (Mark 1:22-28)

In 1:22 Mark tells of a man with an "unclean spirit". For him an "unclean spirit" was an evil force, of demonic origin; he used the terms "unclean spirit" and "demon" synonymously and with equal frequency. At the time illness, and particularly mental illness, was regularly blamed on the influence of or possession by demonic forces. That view contains the truth that illness does represent a hostile world; today, we view viruses as hostile to the human system. In their fashion, they are "demonic." Later, in Mk 3:22-30, we learn that the exorcisms of Jesus are to be seen in terms of the struggle with Satan begun in the temptation (1:12-13). Each specific exorcism is an instance of the unrelenting hostility between Jesus and the spirit of evil. This is a distinctively apocalyptic viewpoint. A word, then, on apocalyptic.

Apocalyptic

It helps to see apocalyptic in relation to providence and eschatology. The word "providence" comes from the Latin *pro* "before" and *videre*, "to see". Providence has to do with looking ahead, seeing what is before one. The providence of God means that God sees and directs the whole course of history. Eschatology, from the Greek *eschaton*, "final", "the end", means that God is guiding history to a final goal. Apocalyptic affirms that God will bring about the final goal in the near future. His purpose has been secretly revealed (the Greek *apocalypsis* means "revelation") to a seer and will be made known.

In apocalyptic thought, it is taken for granted that a supernatural world stands above our earthly world. That heavenly world is the "real" world. There is, indeed, a twofold dualism: vertical – the world above and our world, horizontal – our age and the age to come. In short, the presumption is of an otherworldly reality which dictates the fate of our world. There is a looking to life beyond death, a life very different from the life of our experience. There is always a definitive eschatological judgment: the final clash between Good and Evil, issuing in the total victory of Good (God) and the end of Evil.

In the here and now the grim struggle goes on. There is, in our world, an oppressive burden of evil. Awful things happen every day. "Satan" is a powerful symbol (see Rev 12:3-4, 13-18), representing the whole gamut of evil and its infectious presence in the human race. The Christian life is the restoration of all things in Christ – meaning the absolute end of evil itself. The exorcisms of Jesus are to be viewed in terms of an apocalyptic struggle. They show the inbreak of the rule of God.

Exorcism at Capernaum (1:22-28)

Two distinct episodes are set in the Capernaum synagogue (1:22-28): a teaching of Jesus which provoked the admiration of his hearers, and the expulsion of an unclean spirit which awoke reverential fear in the bystanders. Jesus is powerful in deed and word. "He cried out" (1:24) – the Greek uses a strong word meaning "to cry aloud," "to shout": the demon shouts brazenly at Jesus. "What have you to do with us?" – what is Jesus doing meddling in the domain of evil? "Have you come to destroy us?" – a defiant accusation. "I know who you are" – an attempt to gain magic power over Jesus by uttering his secret name: the "Holy One of God". Recognition of Jesus as God's agent is common among the demons (3:11). This demon acknowledged, besides, that Jesus' mission was designed to destroy the demonic power-structure. Ironically, it was an "unclean spirit" that drew attention to who Jesus is and the ultimate purpose of his coming. No human, before the cross (see 15:39), recognized that Jesus was Son of God; "demons" were thought to have preternatural knowledge. We twentieth-century Christians have a worldview very different from that of our brother Mark – very different from that of our brother Jesus of Nazareth. We join with Mark in acknowledging, in our manner, that Jesus Christ is Lord.

Jesus "rebuked" or "strictly charged" (epitimaó, v 25) the spirit: in the New Testament the word means a formal command that has to be obeyed. Hostility was mutual: a defiant shout (v 24) was answered by a stern command: "Be silent," literally, "be muzzled" (the verb is used again in addressing the storm, 4:39): the arrogant spirit is being told to "shut up" (v 25). Jesus' word of command (and word was enough) produced convulsions and shouting (v 26). This was more than a manifestation of spiteful rage: the exorcism stories show a contrast (implicit here) between a demon's violence and hurtfulness towards a person possessed and the gentleness of Jesus and his communion with a liberated person (see 9:26-27; 5:2-5,15). The extreme amazement (v 27) of those present was occasioned by the authoritative teaching and the effortless exorcism. Expressions of astonishment at the actions of, or before the person of Jesus are frequent throughout Mark. It is the evangelist's way of drawing the attention of the reader to a manifestation of Jesus' true status. The crowds were amazed because they did not understand what was really taking place and who it was who stood before them. The Christian reader must not miss the full import of the text.

The Gerasene demoniac (5:1-20)

This narrative is skilfully presented as a little drama in four acts. The interest shifts from the afflicted man (vv 1-10), to the herd of swine (vv 11-13), then to the people of the area (vv 14-17), and back again to the man and Jesus by the lakeside (vv 18-20). The core of 5:1-20 is an exorcism story which has been embellished with folkloristic details. It can readily be seen that the episode of the swine is not essential to the main story. For the evangelist, however, the resultant dramatic narrative was full of meaning. For this was no ordinary exorcism. The man was victim of an unusually severe case of demonic possession (vv 2-5), explained in terms of multiple possession (v 9) – in our terms, he was violently insane. All goes to demonstrate the overweening power of Jesus which not only rid the man of his evil guests, but cleansed the land of them (vv 10-13). The afflicted one's fellow citizens were witness to the extraordinary power that had been at work (vv 14-17). The exorcism had taken place in Gentile territory (Decapolis); in this land, cleansed by Jesus himself, the healed man became a precursor, heralding the preaching of the good news to the Gentiles (vv 18-20).

The descriptive passage 5:3-5 carries the stamp of Mark's vocabu-

lary. Its vividness serves to underline the importance of the incident. The demoniac "bowed down" before Jesus: the evil spirit was
conscious of the presence of an exceptional spiritual force. In the
story line, invocation of the name "Jesus, Son of the Most High
God" (v 7) was probably a despairing attempt to counter the power
of the exorcist. It was the evangelist's view, however, that demons,
with preternatural insight, perceived something of the true standing of Jesus. "The Most High God," a Gentile designation of the
God of Israel (see Dan 3:26; 4:2; Acts 16:17), came fittingly from a
Gentile demon. "I adjure you by God" was a formula employed in
Jewish exorcisms; there is irony in its use here by a demon in
addressing Jesus. "Do not torment me" (v 7) – Matthew (8:29) has
caught the implication: "Have you come here to torment us before
the time?" The unclean spirit recognized that definitive torment
awaited it.

The tables were turned on the demon: Jesus demanded to know its
name and won an instant response (v 9). "Legion" implies that a
host of demons had invaded the man. In line with the view that illness was due to evil influences, it is understandable that, popularly,
it was believed that a person so fearsomely insane must have been
assaulted by a very regiment of baneful forces. Other examples of
possession by more than one demon are: Lk 8:2; Mt 12:45; (Mk 16:9).
Demons, in popular opinion, were thought to be attached to a particular locality from which they were reluctant to be banished; see
Lk 11:24. Here, the demon had surrendered and was now pleading
desperately for terms (Mk 5:10). The episode of the pigs is patently
folk narrative with typical earthy humor. The demons had, seemingly, won a concession, but it proved to be their undoing. We are
to take it that they perished with the pigs. No Jew would have shed
a tear over the destruction of a herd of pigs – fitting habitat for
demons indeed! For Mark the drowning was important as he shows
his reader that the episode went far beyond the deliverance of the
unhappy possessed one. It was expulsion of a horde of demons
from the land, a veritable victory of Jesus in the domain of Satan.

The scene changes (vv 14-20). It is not surprising (as the narrative
runs) that the herdsmen fled, nor that people hastened to verify
their startling story. These newcomers were filled with superstit-
ious terror of Jesus' awesome power. The contrast of v 15 with vv 3-5

is typical of exorcism stories: the contrast between the violence and destructiveness of the demonic spirit and the tranquillity of the liberated person. The concluding verses 18-20 are theologically eloquent for Mark. The man begged that "he might be with" Jesus, that is, that he might become a disciple. Jesus' refusal of the man's generous gesture made in thankfulness was by no means ungracious; nor, for that matter, was it really a refusal. He would not take the man with him in his immediate circle of disciples because he had a special mission for him: he was to be the first missionary to the Gentiles. And that is why, though the man was bidden to tell what God had done for him (v 19), what he in fact did was to "proclaim" (see 1:14; 3:14) the deed of Jesus. The notion of the Christian message to the Gentiles is close to the surface.

The Gentile woman (7:24-30)

For Mark, the presence of Jesus in the region of Tyre, a Gentile area bordering on north-western Galilee, and his healing wrought for a Gentile woman, carried great weight. The focus of the story is the dialogue between Jesus and the woman; the exorcism is secondary. The saying of Jesus, "It is not fair to take the childrens' food and throw it to the dogs" (v 27) shows him acknowledging the distinction between Jew and Gentile as of God's design. Jesus, in fact, did limit his ministry to "the house of Israel" (see Mt 15:24). The woman will not be put off by Jesus' refusal: all very well indeed – but even the dogs get crumbs! And Jesus responded to the challenge. This quick-witted woman appealed to his sense of humour. From the vantage point of successful Gentile mission, Mark had modified the saying by prefacing, "Let the children (i.e. Jews) be fed first;" in his day the turn of the Gentiles had come. He had found a trace of a "Gentile mission" of Jesus, but he did not dissemble how faint a trace.

The woman was "a Gentile, of Syrophoenician origin" (7:26) – a Gentile both by religion and by birth, a representative of the Gentile world. The suppliant's little daughter had an unclean spirit: Mark's predilection for exorcism stories. Jesus' refusal (v 27) was cleverly trumped by the woman (v 28). He bowed to the woman's faith and assured her that her child was already healed. If Jesus had yielded to this cry of faith even while the division between Jew and Gentile still stood (see Eph 2:11-12), how much more, Mark seems to say, must the Christian church go out to Gentiles now that Jesus had laid down his life as a ransom "for many" (Mk 10:45), had poured out his blood "for many" (14:24).

The indications are that Mark 7:24-8:26 was planned to meet the interest of Gentile-Christian readers. Mark wanted to show that the concern of Jesus, despite the constraint of his mission, was not limited to Jews but reached to non-Jewish peoples, beyond the confines of Galilee. When one examines more closely the topographical references in 7:24 and 7:31, one finds that it was Mark who engineered this brief venture of Jesus beyond Jewish territory. Apart from this and the Gerasene demoniac episode (5:1-20), Mark has given only an intimation, expressed in terms of journeys across the lake, of a ministry of Jesus to Gentiles. But that was enough for him to show that the door had been opened to them.

An epileptic boy (9:14-29)

Mark has purposely placed the narrative of the epileptic demoniac directly after the transfiguration (9:2-13). As the heavenly acknowledgment of Jesus at the baptism (1:11) was followed by Satan's temptation (1:12-13) so, too, the acknowledgment at the transfiguration (9:7) was followed by Jesus' encounter with a demon. The editorial verses 9:14-16 are a bridge from the transfiguration to the healing of the epileptic. The central theme is the powerlessness of the disciples: Jesus was absent and nothing went right for them. They were unable to cope with an evil spirit and surely would have been out of their depth in theological debate with scribes (9:14-18).

In 9:18a the distressing symptoms of epilepsy are described (see v 20) – the recurrent convulsions and fits being ascribed to periodical assault by an evil spirit. "They were not able" – Mark underlines the disciples' inability: not only the petitioner, but they themselves (v 28), were surprised to find that they were powerless. After all, they had been granted power over unclean spirits (6:7,13). "You faithless generation" (9:19) is an echo of Dt 32:5 (see Mk 8:12). The reproof is general and expresses the weariness of Jesus in face of the lack of faith manifested by his contemporaries – including the disciples.

Jesus' question, "How long has this been happening to him?" (v 21a) serves to bring out the gravity of the malady (vv 21b-22). The seizure could have come upon the boy at any time, so he could have toppled into fire or water; the father attributed this to the malevolent spite of the evil spirit. "But if you are able to do anything" – the man had been discouraged by the failure of the disciples. "If you are able!" – Jesus fixed upon the lack of faith. "All things can be done for one who believes": not that faith can do everything, but that faith will set no limits to the power of God. "I believe, help my unbelief!" (v 24) – the father admitted that his faith was defective. For its strengthening and growth it required the help of the Master – the Christian overtones are obvious. With this cry from the heart the man emerged in a favourable light and stood in contrast to the disciples.

The baneful spirit was not only expelled but was bidden, "never enter him again!" (v 25). Since the affliction was not continuous but recurrent the spirit must not only leave but must not return. "Like a corpse" (v 26): the boy lay motionless and pallid; most of the crowd took him for dead. "Took him by the hand" (see 1:31; 5:41), "lifted him up" (see 1:31), "he arose" (see 5:42) – the parallels with the healing of Peter's mother-in-law (1:29-31) and the raising of Jairus' daughter (5:35-43) are evident and deliberate. The technical language of the early church's preaching of the death and resurrection of Christ is even more marked in the present passage. The kerygmatic intent is more obvious, coming in the middle of a section dominated by predictions of the passion and resurrection (8:31-32; 9:30-32). The cure, worked by Jesus, was a symbol and a presage of resurrection from the dead. The theme comes dramatically here after the disciples' questioning about the meaning of rising from the dead (9:10).

In vv 28-29 Jesus was alone with the disciples "in a house" and they questioned him "privately" – the Greek phrase *kat' idian* being an unmistakable Marcan label. This esoteric message to the disciples is, in reality, addressed to the Christian community. Jesus explained why the disciples had been unable to cope with the unclean spirit: prayer was vitally necessary because the exorcist must rely wholly on the power of God. Some manuscripts add "and fasting" (v 28). Its addition is understandable but wrongheaded – it misses the point of the story. Fasting would introduce something of one's own effort, whereas the point being precisely made is total reliance on the Lord.

This is the final exorcism story in Mark and the only one in the second part of the gospel. The motif of faith is firmly stressed. Jesus upraided the faithless generation: all – scribes and Pharisees, the people, the very disciples – have been without understanding and hardhearted. And the boy's father had doubted the power of Jesus: "If you are able!" He was told that faith does not set limits to the power of God. His cry is the heart of the story: he acknowledged his lack of faith and looked to Jesus for help. At that moment he stood in sharp contrast to the Twelve who displayed their lack of trust. Jesus lifted up one who looked like a corpse, who was reckoned to be dead. Now the disciples learned what rising from the dead meant (9:10): Christ's victory over the forces of evil. Now they recognized the power and authority of Jesus. Only through union with their Master in prayer will they participate in that same power. Bereft of his presence, stripped of communion with him, Christians are powerless and helpless.

The outsider exorcist (9:38-40)

The practice of exorcism was widespread in the Hellenistic period among both Jews and Gentiles. See Acts 19:13-16. The episode of an exorcist who was not a disciple is linked to the preceding passage by the catchword "in my name", here meaning an exorcism worked by invocation of the name of Jesus. The exorcist was "not following us", that is, not a disciple. The fact of casting out demons "in the name of Jesus" shows that the exorcist acknowledged the authority of Jesus; he was not opposed to Jesus and his disciples even if he was not part of them. The saying of Jesus – "No one who does a deed of power in my name will be able soon afterward to speak evil of me" (v 39) – offered his disciples a directive: they were not to forbid one who acts so. In the context it was a matter of sucessful exorcism: the person, was "casting out demons" (v 38) and Jesus spoke of a "mighty work" done by invocation of his name. The presumption is that one who performs a good deed in the name of Jesus cannot be an enemy of his. The saying of v 40 – "Whoever is not against us is for us" – suits the context perfectly. In a Christian setting the statement means that one belongs in Jesus' church as long as one does not categorically separate oneself from him.

CONCLUSION

The exorcisms of Jesus were, in fact, healings. The difference between them and the recognized healings is that in the exorcism the current view that human ills were due to evil forces that warred against us was more pronounced. And in them, too, the apocalyptic dimension was more present. Here, more than elsewhere, we face the fact that Jesus of Nazareth was, authentically, a first-century Jew. When the author of Hebrews declared that Jesus "had to become like his brothers and sisters in every respect" (2:17) he really meant it. Every human is influenced by his or her culture. We are people of our age, no matter how well we may come to understand people of other times and places. We cannot turn the historical Jesus into a citizen of the twentieth century. Here we strive to see him through the eyes of Mark. It remains a first-century perspective. Our concern is to understand the exorcism stories as signs of God's concern for humankind and as promises of God's ultimate and total victory over evil. In Jesus' view they demonstrated that indeed "the kingdom of God is among you" (see Luke 17:21).

A distinctive feature of the exorcism at Capernaum (Mk 1:22-28) was that it not only demonstrated the power of Jesus but served to bolster his teaching authority. In that episode *exousia* was the seed of conflict, for he taught "not as the scribes" (v 22). The religious authorities would see his teaching as threat. They had to discredit his exorcist activity, attributing it to a demonic source (3:22). This was "blasphemy against the Holy Spirit" (3:29). To the extent that we, too, fail to discern in the words and deeds of Jesus the presence of our God, we are guilty of that same "blasphemy." And, indeed, individually and as church, we have been selective in our discernment. When we stress "authoritative" teaching of Jesus we find that words which serve to bolster institution have been taken very seriously indeed. What a structure has been raised on the isolated "Petrine text" – which occurs only in Mt 16:17-19. Another Matthean text, emphatically excluding rank and honorific titles (23:8-10) has simply been ignored. More importantly, Jesus' startling reinterpretation of authority – Mk 10:42-45 – has not been taken to heart. There may well be a barbed message for our day in Mark's association of authority and exorcism. "It is not so among you" (10:43): we need to exorcize the spirit of the world if we are to hearken to this word, and put it into practice.

In the story of the Syrophoenician woman (7:24-30) we are given a precious glimpse into the character of Jesus. He is, once more, a man of his day, going along with the accepted division between Jew and Gentile. His sense of humour, discernible in several of his parables, is here presupposed. Behind his "For saying that" (7:29) one may hear his spontaneous and appreciative laughter – he had been trumped! Mark had observed, beyond the historical confines of his ministry (to Israel), the wider dimension of his mission – to all. The story of the epileptic boy (9:14-29) is a lesson on the growth of faith (9:23-24) and a pointer to the life-giving power of the Risen One (9:26-27). And the explanation to the disciples – "only through prayer" (v 29) – anticipates the declaration of the Johannine Jesus: "Apart from me you can do nothing" (Jn 15:5). The admonition to the jealous John ("and we tried to stop him", 9:38) – "Whoever is not against us is for us" (v 40) – is more than a summons to ecumenism. It is a challenge to see the presence not only of God but of Christ wherever in our world the good is present. See Mt 25:31-45.

CHAPTER 7

Messiah

The Lion of the tribe of Judah, the root of David, has conquered ...
then I saw a Lamb standing as though it had been slain. (Rev 5:5-6).

"The beginning of the good news of Jesus Christ, the Son of God"
(Mk 1:1). This superscription includes two of Mark's significant
christological titles: Christ (Messiah) and Son of God. We look, first,
to the title Messiah. It is quite unlikely that Jesus himself ever
claimed to be the Messiah. It is very likely, on the other hand, that
some of his followers thought him to be the Messiah. It is also very
likely that Jesus' opponents may have understood him or his followers to claim that he was the Messiah. After the resurrection, of
course, Jesus was, by his followers, regularly called the Messiah –
Jesus Christ (Messiah).[18]

THE MESSIAH

Messiah (Mk 8:29-30)

"He asked them, 'But who do you say that I am?' Peter answered
him, 'You are the Messiah.'" In the evangelist's eyes the unique significance of Peter's confession rests upon the fact that here, for the
first time, the disciples told Jesus who, in their estimation, he was.
Jesus took the initiative and questioned the disciples about the
opinion of "people" ("those outside", 4:11) and learned that they
did not regard him as a messianic figure but, at most, as a traditional
forerunner of the Messiah (8:27-28). Peter, however, had at last
begun to see: "You are the Messiah." The sequel will show that his
understanding of Jesus' messiahship was quite wide of the mark.

Mark looked beyond Peter and the disciples to the community of
his concern and bade his Christians take care that they really understood who their Christ is. There had been a studied preparation of
the reader. From the start Mark had shown Jesus acting in an extra-

ordinary manner which called forth the astonishment of the witnesses and led to a series of questions about him (1:27; 2:7; 6:2).
Jesus himself heightened the effect (2:10,28). Who is this Son of Man?
Who is the Physician? (3:16-17). Who is this Bridegroom? (2:19). The
themes of the amazement of the crowd and the incomprehension of
the disciples stand as a question-mark over the first eight chapters
of the gospel. And now, for the Christians who read Mark, the confession, "You are the Messiah" is their profession of faith. The
warning is: that confession might be inadequate (8:32-33).

Son of David (10:47-48)

For Mark the story of 10:46-52 sounds a new departure in the self-
revelation of Jesus. He found himself acclaimed, repeatedly, as
"Son of David." Far from imposing silence, he summoned the blind
man to him and openly restored his sight. "Son of David" is a manifestly messianic title: Jesus is the messianic king, heir of the
promise to David (2 Sam 7:12-16; 1 Chr 17: 11-14; Ps 89:29-38). Jesus
showed implicit approval of the title. There was no need of secrecy.
Emphasis on suffering ever since Caesarea Philippi (8:31) had ruled
out a triumphalist dimension.

Later, while teaching in the temple, Jesus himself raised the Son of
David question: "How can the scribes say that the Messiah is the
Son of David?" (12:35). It might seem that the question was designed
to contest the Davidic descent of the Messiah. Rather, it was meant
as a criticism of the scribes' understanding of Davidic messiahship,
and so of their refusal to acknowledge the true personality of Jesus.
Psalm 110, the opening verse of which is quoted in 12:36, is a royal
psalm, addressed to the king – "my lord" is the king. Sitting at the
right hand of Yahweh means the king's adoption as God's son (his
representative), the acknowledged status of the Davidic king (2
Sam 7:14). The argument here depends on the then current acceptance of the psalm as a composition of David (it is, in fact, later). On
this supposition David presents an oracle of Yahweh addressed to
one whom he entitles "my Lord". The solemn attestation of David
is underlined by the formula, unique in the synoptic gospels,
"[inspired] by the Holy Spirit." This adds weight to the further
question in v 37 – "David himself calls him lord; so how can he be
his son?" If the great David had addressed the Messiah as "Lord"
then the Davidic sonship of the Messiah must be understood in a

sense that will acknowledge his superiority to David. The upshot is that Son of David is not really an adequate title. It does not capture the character of Jesus' messiahship.

Physician (2:17)

The call of Levi (2:14), parallel to the call of the first disciples (1:16-20), serves as an introduction to the pronouncement story 2:15-17. The whole passage (2:13-17) illustrated Jesus' attitude towards outcasts and strikingly brought to the fore the amply attested fact that Jesus' concern for outcasts was a scandal to the religious authorities. We know that table fellowship (between Christians of Jewish and Gentile backgrounds) was something of a problem in the early church (see Acts 11:3; Gal 2:12); it would have been crucial in the matter of eucharistic table fellowship. It may well be that this interest accounts for the formation and preservation of the original story.

For the evangelist, however, the episode was closely associated with the preceding cure of the paralytic (2:1-12). There the centre of interest was the authority of the Son of Man to forgive sins; here it is the presence of the "Physician" able to "cure" the "sick," that is, sinners. The fact that Jesus associated with sinners was a sign not only of the remission of sins but of the presence of one who could remit sins. In the Old Testament, Yahweh alone is the Physician, the Healer (see Hosea 14:4; Jer 3:22; 17;4; 30:17; Sir 38:1-15), and healing is a sign of the messianic age (see Is 61:1; Mt 10:1,8). Against this background, Jesus' reference to himself as "physician" – "Those who are well have no need of a physician, but those who are sick; I have come to call not the righteous but sinners" – implied more than a proverbial justification of his conduct. If he ate with sinners it was because the sick had need of the Physician. For those who could see, his calculated practice of breaking bread with sinners was a declaration that the kingdom had indeed "come near" (1:15): the Physician was at work.

Friend of sinners

Virtually everything that the early church remembered about John the Baptist had to do with repentance in view of imminent judgment. But with Jesus we have a different emphasis. There is the summary statement that Jesus preached repentance in view of the nearness of the kingdom: "The time is fulfilled, and the kingdom of God has come near; repent and believe in the good news" (Mk 1:15). While there is a summons to repent, it is surely not the whole message. Indeed, there is not a significant body of reliable material that explicitly attributes to Jesus a call for general, or for national, repentance in view of the coming kingdom. What is surprising is that, while looking for the restoration of Israel, he did not follow the majority and urge the traditional means toward that end: repentance and return to observance of the law.

Jesus himself was not primarily a preacher of repentance; he proclaimed the imminent coming of the kingdom as salvation. The parables of God seeking the lost (Lk 15:3-6, 8-9), once Luke's conclusions (15:7,10) are removed, can be seen as focused not on repentance but on God's initiative and action. The one distinctive note that we can be certain marked Jesus' teaching about the kingdom is that it would include the "sinners". There should be no confusion about the basic meaning of the term "sinners" in the gospels. It comes from the Hebrew *resha'im* – the wicked: those who sinned wilfully and did not repent. The Septuagint (the Greek Old Testament) rendered *resha'im* by *hamartóloi* ("sinners") and Greek-speaking Jews used the term of the non-observant who had placed themselves outside of the covenant. The "sinners" of the gospels are these "wicked" people regarded as living blatantly outside the Law. Jesus saw his mission as being to "the lost" and the "sinners", that is, to the wicked. He was also concerned with the poor, the meek, and the downtrodden. If there was conflict, it was about the status of the wicked: "This fellow welcomes sinners and even eats with them!" Jesus was accused of associating with and offering the kingdom to those who by the normal standards of Judaism were wicked.

We can clearly state what repentance would normally have involved. By ordinary Jewish standards, offences against others required reparation as well as repentance. In Jesus' time, repentance would be demonstrated by sacrifice in the temple (e.g. Lev 6:1-5). Jesus offered sinners inclusion in the kingdom not only while they were still sinners but also without requiring repentance. Therefore he could have been accused of being a friend of people who remained sinners. For Jesus to welcome repentant sinners who had made amends, would have been quite acceptable to the "righteous" –

whatever else they may have thought of Jesus. The scandal was that he associated with sinners and rejoiced in their company. He asked only that they accept his message – which offered them the kingdom. This was the scandal of the righteous.

Bridegroom (Mark 2:19-20)

The passage 2:19-22 is made up of a pronouncement story (2:18-20) to which two sayings, on patches and wineskins, have been added (2:21-22). The main story manifests, yet again, the presence of the kingdom: the fact that the disciples of Jesus did not fast brought home to those who could understand that the Bridegroom was with them. This was, already, a Christian claim. While the image of wedding feast expressed the joy of the messianic age, neither in the Old Testament nor in early Judaism was the Messiah represented as bridegroom. On the other hand, Yahweh was cast as spouse of his covenant people (see Hos 2:19; Is 54: 3-6; 62:5; Jer 2:2; Ezek 16). Jesus' implied claim to be bridegroom is a claim on par with that of authority to forgive sins (Mk 2:10).

If Jesus was bridegroom, then he had ushered in the joyful time of salvation. His disciples were guests at a wedding feast; it was surely not the time or place for fasting. Indeed, during his ministry, "they cannot fast"! (v 19). Jesus was equivalently claiming that, in his ministry, the kingdom was already present. And there is a further factor. It is important to note that Jesus was replying to a question put to him by outsiders – "people" (v 18). His reply not only explained why, unlike groups such as the Baptist's followers and the Pharisees, his disciples did not fast; it asserted the distinctiveness of his group.

> What is unheard of is for some individual Jewish teacher to tell outsiders that what marks off his disciples from every other pious Jewish group is that in principle his disciples cannot fast at all because of his particular message and ministry. In effect, then, at least on this one issue of voluntary fasting, Jesus distinguished his disciples from all other Jews.[19]

Jesus was thereby making a remarkable claim for his own person and ministry.

But Mark has a problem. Despite the known praxis of Jesus it is evident that fasting had become a practice among Christians. He has to produce a relevant codicil (v 20) to the declaration of Jesus. The bridegroom was manifestly Jesus and his being "taken away" was a veiled reference to his impending death. It is an echo of Is 53:8 – "By a perversion of justice he was taken away." The eschatological prophecy ("the days will come") of Mk 2:20, put in the mouth of Jesus, announced, in place of the present wedding atmosphere, a time of bereavement: Jesus will no longer be physically present. If, at present, they cannot fast, then they will fast. A practice of fasting, current in Mark's day, has been duly justified.

MESSIAH OF JEW AND GENTILE

"He went up the mountain and called to him those whom he wanted" (3:13). This was a solemn moment. Luke had thoroughly grasped the significance of it and had emphasized the choice of the twelve by specifying the night-long prayer of Jesus (Lk 6:12). For Mark, "the mountain" was the setting for a sovereign deed of Jesus. From out of the enthusiastic crowd he proceeded to make a choice of those "whom he wanted." In view of 15:40-41, with its reference to the women who "used to follow him and provided for him when he was in Galilee" – "many other women" besides the three named – it surely must be that some "whom he wanted, and they came to him" were women.

Within the chosen group "he appointed twelve" (3:14). The Twelve had a symbolic role: they stood for a renewed Israel – renewal of Israel was the mission of Jesus. The symbol was fixed: twelve tribes sprung from twelve sons. The symbolic Twelve had to be men – Jesus had no choice there. The disciples were a wider group. The often repeated statement, "Jesus chose only men," is demonstrably false. Jesus' disciples were men and women.

Bread of the Banquet (Mk 6:35-44; 8:1-9; see 14:22-25)

All four gospels carry the story of the multiplication of loaves; Mark (6:35-44; 8:1-10) and Matthew (14:13-21; 15:29-38) have two accounts of a miraculous feeding. There are several arguments for regarding these two accounts in Mark and Matthew as variant forms of the same incident. Luke (9:10-17) follows Mark 6:32-44. It seems best to take it that the fourth evangelist (John 6:1-15) drew on an independent tradition like that of Mark's and Matthew's second account.

In the teaching tradition of the Christian community the relevance of the multiplication of loaves to the eucharist, the bread of God's people, was quickly recognized. We find close parallels in gesture and wording between both synoptic accounts and the narratives of the Last Supper. "While they were eating, he took a loaf of bread, and after blessing it he broke it, gave it to them..." (14:22). Compare: "Taking the five loaves ... he blessed and broke the loaves, and gave ... (6:41); "He took the seven loaves ... and after giving thanks he broke them and gave ..." (8:6). And it was only at the feeding miracle and the last Supper that Jesus explicitly acted as host of a meal. John's account, too, shows some adaptation (Jn 6:4-14). And, of course, in his plan, the multiplication of loaves was the starting point of the Bread of Life discourses. It is evident, then, that the story of the feeding was treasured in the early communities not only because it related a mighty work of Jesus, but also because of its symbolic relation to the eucharist.

The story of Jesus feeding the multitude has association not only with the eucharist but also with a meal pattern throughout the ministry. Matthew 11:18-19 sets up a contrast between the Baptist and Jesus: "John came neither eating nor drinking ... the Son of Man came eating and drinking, and they say, 'Look, a glutton and a drunkard, a friend of tax collectors and sinners!'" The saying presupposes a well-established reputation. Jesus, unlike the Baptist, was no ascetic. This squares with Jesus' contention that, as long as he was with them, his disciples cannot fast (Mk 2:19). Reference to tax collectors and sinners is important. Jesus showed his concern for the socially despised and for "sinners" (non-observant Jews on a par with Gentiles) precisely through table fellowship with them. Thus, in Mk 2:16, the challenge of the Pharisees to the disciples, "Why does he eat with tax collectors and sinners?" and the note of exasperation, if not of disgust, in Lk 15:2 – "And the Pharisees and the scribes were grumbling, and saying, 'This fellow welcomes sinners and eats with them!'"

We may find the key to Jesus' understanding of his practice of table fellowship with outcasts in Mt 8:11 – "I tell you, many will come from east and west and will eat with Abraham and Isaac and Jacob in the kingdom of heaven" (see Lk 13:28). His shared meals were a preparation for and an anticipation of the final banquet in the king-

dom. Moreover, in table fellowship with sinners Jesus was display-
ing the Father's preferential option for sinners (see Lk 15:7,10). If,
then, at the Last Supper, Jesus asserted that his next drink of wine
would be at table in the fulness of the kingdom, he implied that the
Supper was the climax of a series of meals which celebrated, in
anticipation, the joy of the banquet. They were meals which,
indeed, opened the banquet to all who would not deliberately reject
the invitation. It is against this rich background we may expect to
understand the story of the feeding. The view of John P. Meier is
persuasive:

> It is within this greater context and regular habit of Jesus' public
> ministry, a habit that culminated with what was literally the
> Last Supper among a great number of "suppers," that one may
> try to understand the origin of the story of the feeding miracle.
> In my opinion, the criterion of both multiple attestation and
> coherence make it likely that, amid the various celebrations of
> table fellowship Jesus hosted during his ministry, there was one
> especially memorable one: memorable because of the unusual
> number of participants, memorable also because, unlike many
> meals held in towns and villages, this one was held by the Sea of
> Galilee. In contrast to Jesus' other "kingdom meals," bread and
> fish rather than bread and wine (cf Mt 11:18-19 par.; Mk 14:22-
> 25) would be the natural components of such a meal at such a
> spot. Connected from the beginning with Jesus' eschatological
> message, this special meal of bread and fish, shared by a large
> crowd by the Sea of Galilee, would be remembered and inter-
> preted by the post Easter church through the filter of the Last
> Supper tradition and the church's own celebration of the
> eucharist. [20]

In Mark one may discern a further dimension. The two Marcan
feeding narratives have much in common but also carry some
notable differences. Both are set in a "desert place," the second
more explicitly so, and evoke the Exodus and the manna, bread
from God. Both, in the description of the miracle (the evangelist
does think of miracle), stress the size of the crowd, and food so
abundant that a large amount was left over. Both end with the dismissal of the crowd and a journey by boat. We are, beyond doubt,
in the presence of a literary doublet. But Mark chose to see two sep-

arate incidents. The indications are that he viewed the feeding of the five thousand as a sign to Jews and the feeding of the four thousand as a sign to Gentiles. Already, in 7:27-28 (the encounter with the Syrophoenician woman) there is a plea that the Gentiles, too, be allowed to participate, to a limited extent at least, in God's bounty. But now it is no longer a question of their being permitted to glean crumbs: the disciples are to give them of the abundance of the table (8:8).

In 6:43-44, five thousand had been fed and twelve baskets of the fragments of bread and fish were collected; in 8:8-9 four thousand were fed and seven baskets of fragments were collected. The differences are obvious but Mark has given us a pointer as to which are, for him, the significant variants: the baskets of fragments (see 8:19-20). For, there is no denying that Mark does strikingly draw attention to the two feeding stories, deliberately repeating the numbers "twelve" and "seven" and using again (see 6:43; 8:8) two different words for basket: *cophinos*, a basket commonly used by Jews and *spyris*, an ordinary basket. Besides, he has insinuated that the first feeding is in a Jewish setting, the other in a Gentile setting (see 7:31). Mark is no careless writer. These details, for him, are meaningful and, in the setting of this section of his gospel (6:35-8:26), we are justified in seeing in them deliberate pointers to Jewish and Gentile components of his Christian community.

Mark had, throughout, stressed the failure of the twelve to understand (4:13,40-41; 6:52; 7:18; 8:4); in all cases they displayed lack of spiritual insight in failing to discern some hidden meaning in a word or deed of Jesus. The passage 8:14-21 is the climax of this theme in the first half of the gospel. A series of seven questions conveys Jesus' bitter disappointment at their tardiness. "Do you not yet understand?" is the burden of his censure. Mark wrote with the special needs of his community in mind; therefore he has exaggerated the obtuseness of the disciples. The drama of the episode is present from the first: "Now the disciples had forgotten to bring any bread; and they had only one loaf with them in the boat!" (v 41). The disciples, who had been actively involved in two miraculous feedings, where Jesus had satisfied the needs of great crowds, were now concerned because they were short of bread! They "had only one loaf with them in the boat" – this is not just a vivid Marcan touch. The development of the passage will suggest that what the disciples failed to understand was that Jesus is the one loaf for Jews and Gentiles – as the feedings ought to have shown them (see 1 Cor 10:16-17; 12:12-13).

Bracketed by the repeated, "Do you not understand?" (vv 17, 21), the specific recalling of the two feedings is marked as the key factor of the passage. The unexpected emphasis – on the baskets of fragments – is a further indication that this is just where we must look. We are meant to see that the number (twelve) and the *cophinos*, a basket commonly used by Jews, point to the Jewish world, while the number seven (universal) and the ordinary basket (*spyris*) indicate the Gentile world. Those of Gentile background as well as those of Jewish origin are both at home in the household of the faith. And their fellowship is achieved in the breaking of the bread. The Christian who cannot or will not see this merits the charge: is your heart hardened? It would appear that Mark has some Jewish-Christian disciples primarily in view. The kind of situation that Paul encountered in Jerusalem and Antioch (Galatians 2) would also have cropped up again at a later date in other areas. It would not have been easy for Pharisaic Jews, coming to Christianity, to shrug off their ingrained prejudice and enter into warm fellowship with Gentiles. Jesus, the "one loaf", was the Messiah uniting Jew and Gentile about himself into one messianic people.

THE WAY OF THE MESSIAH

Messianic entry (11:1-11)

For Mark's readers the coming of Jesus to Jerusalem had an evident messianic significance. It is not unlikely that the episode happened not at Passover but at a feast of Dedication, and Mark's narrative suggests that it was a modest affair: the immediate disciples and Jesus riding in their midst. It was a prophetic gesture. Nothing would have been more commonplace than a man riding a donkey; and a small group of pilgrims, waving branches and shouting acclamations from Psalm 118 would not have occasioned a second glance at the feast of Dedication (*Hanukkah*). Yet, whatever others might have thought, those who could see (certainly, Christian readers of the gospel) perceived that this entry to Jerusalem (as it is here presented) was the solemn entry of the Saviour-King into his city. Jesus himself took the initiative: he would enter as the King of Zechariah 9:9 – where it is Yahweh, as divine warrior, who rides into Jerusalem. In Mark there is a studied reticence. The text of Zech 9:9

is not quoted (cf Mt 21:5); there are no "crowds" (Mt 21:9), no "multitude" (Lk 19:37,39); the people had not actually acclaimed Jesus as "Son of David" (cf Mt 21:9) though they had spread their cloaks and leafy branches for his passage. In this entry to Jerusalem Jesus himself, for the first time in the gospel, made a messianic gesture – but in a special manner, wholly in keeping with his destiny of one who had come to serve and to lay down his life.

Despite the "many" of v 8, Mark does not give the impression that the accompanying crowd was large; yet they walked before and after Jesus, forming a procession. "Blessed is the coming kingdom of our father David!" – the acclamation is directed to the kingdom and not to Jesus. Contrast Matthew (21:9): "Hosanna to the Son of David." The entry as depicted in Mark meant the coming of a Messiah who was poor, an advent in humility, not in glory. What was at stake, for Jesus, was the nature and manner of his messiahship. At this moment, come to the city that would so soon witness his passion and death, he could manifest himself. But he did not come as a temporal ruler or with worldly pomp. He came as a religious figure (in his distinctive understanding of religion), a prince of peace, "humble and riding on a donkey" (Zech 9:9). Mark's narrative in 11:11 is consistent with his modest presentation in 11:1-10 and may reflect what really took place, or something like it. Jesus entered the temple by himself ("he entered"), unobserved; the procession seemed to have petered out before the actual entry. His "looking around" involved a critical scrutiny which set the stage for the next episode (11:12-25).

Suffering (Mark 8:32-33; 9:31-32; 10:33-34)

"He said all this quite openly" (8:32) might be rendered: "and openly he proclaimed the word." This was the turning-point in the self-revelation of Jesus. If he still charged his disciples not to reveal his messianic identity (v 30), he now spoke to them quite openly of his messianic destiny of suffering and death. This emphatic affirmation that Jesus spoke openly (parrésia, see Jn 7:26; 10:24) of his passion shows the unusual character of the fact. Even when he had spoken "privately" with his disciples, he had never spoken so clearly. Here it is impossible to miss the meaning of his words, and Peter's reaction (v 32b) shows that he had at once understood what Jesus had said, even though the divine necessity for the suffering escaped him altogether.

"And Peter took him aside": we can picture him, in his earnestness, taking hold of Jesus, and "rebuked" him. The notion of a suffering Messiah was entirely foreign to Peter. He realized, too, that his own situation would be effected: disciple of a suffering Messiah was not a role he relished. The phrase "and looking at his disciples" is proper to Mark: the rebuke is addressed to them as well as Peter. "Get behind me, Satan!" (*hypage opisó mou*, Satana) – the words recall Matt 4:10, "Begone, Satan!" (*hypage*, Satana). This would suggest that Mark knew a form of the Matthew / Luke temptation story. The temptation in the wilderness (Mt 4:1-11; Lk 4:1-13) aimed at getting Jesus himself to conform to a popularly envisaged messianic role, to become a political messiah. It was an attempt to undermine his full acceptance of the will of God for him and here Peter was playing Satan's role. Peter's acknowledgment of Jesus as Messiah had, in principle, set him apart from "people" (v 27); but now Peter found himself rebuked for judging in an all too human manner. Peter, and all like him, who set their minds "on human things," stand opposed to God's purpose and align themselves with Satan.

Jesus had challenged the ambitious brothers, James and John, to consider whether they had really understood what following him involved: "Are you able to drink the cup that I drink, or be baptized with the baptism that I am baptized with?" (10:38). In the Old Testament "cup" is a symbol both of joy (Ps 74:9; Is 43:2; Job 9:31) and of suffering (Ps 74:9; Is 51:17-22; Jer 32:1; Ezek 33:31-34); our context demands the latter sense and, specifically, the idea of redemptive messianic suffering (see Mk 8:31; 9:31; 14:36; Jn 18:11). "The baptism with which I am baptized" (Mk 10:39) – immersion in waters ("baptism") is a metaphor for overwhelming calamity and suffering (Ps 42:7; Is 43:2; Job 9:31). Matthew (20:23) has omitted the clause, but Luke has an instructive parallel: "I have a baptism with which to be baptized, and what stress I am under until it is completed!" The "baptism" is the passion which will "plunge" Jesus into a sea of suffering. Here the brothers are being told: you do not know the price that must be paid to share my glory. Here indeed it is like Master, like servant – Jesus must suffer these things before entering into his glory (Lk 24:26). They must be prepared to accept the full implication of following Jesus.

The second part of Jesus' answer (v 40) concerned, more directly, their demand for the first places in the kingdom. But it is an evasive answer. Jesus is not empowered to grant these places to whom he pleases; they have already been allotted (by God). The appointment of places in the kingdom is at the Father's disposition only; discipleship does not entitle one to receive a special reward nor to make any demand. As in 13:32 Jesus' words imply a subordination to the Father.

Glory –Transfiguration (9:2-8)

The transfiguration episode ranks with the baptism (1:9-1) and Gethsemane (14:32-42) narratives and shows similarities with both. While it is no longer possible to say what transpired upon the mountain – was it vision? was it profound religious experience? – we must seek to understand what the episode meant for Mark. It certainly was important for him. Perhaps his pointer immediately before (9:1) to the kingdom of God coming with power may help us to understand his purpose. A feature of the coming kingdom will be the glorious advent of the Son of Man (see 13:24-27); the transfiguration was, in some sort, a preview of it: a dramatic promise of fulfilment. The Transfiguration (v 2), involving a change in Jesus' form, would be an anticipated glimpse of his glorious state. In v 4 the order Elijah and Moses (Moses and Elijah is the traditional order) is unusual; it may simply be because Mark will go on to speak of the second Elijah (the Baptist, vv 11-13). "Talking with Jesus" (v 4) – Luke gives the theme of the conversation: the "departure" (literally, the *exodos* or death; see Wisdom 3:2; 7:6; 2 Peter 1:15) of Jesus at Jerusalem.

Luke's narrative (Lk 9:28-32) may be a pointer to the basic episode. In the entire first part of Luke's text Jesus held centre stage. He went up on a mountain, site of divine manifestation. He became absorbed in prayer and in the immediacy of communion with God his countenance was altered and his raiment shone with heavenly brightness. "Two men" (Moses and Elijah) appeared to him and spoke with him of his "departure." Moses and Elijah stand for Law and Prophets, the Scripture of Israel. Later, the risen Lord will open the minds of the Emmaus disciples "to understand the scriptures", that is, everything written about him in "the law of Moses, the prophets and the psalms" (Lk 24:44-45). In other words, on the mountain, Jesus himself, through prayerful meditation on the scriptures, in an ineffable mystical experience, came to understand that his destiny was to suffer and to die.

In Mark, however, the aspect of revelation to Jesus yields wholly to the theme of revelation granted to the disciples. And now the entire first part of his narrative prepares for this. Jesus led the three disciples "up a high mountain" where he was transfigured "before them" (Mk 9:2). Elijah and Moses appeared "to them" and it was for the disciples' benefit that a heavenly voice was heard, speaking of Jesus in the third person (9:7). "It is good for us to be here" (v 5) – that is to say, this is a happy moment which ought to be prolonged. The three "dwellings", one each for Jesus, Elijah and Moses, would have put all three on an equal footing. Peter really "did not know what to say;" he has, yet again, totally misunderstood. The voice from heaven set the record straight. "This is my Son, the Beloved" – in contrast to 1:11 (the baptism), the words are here addressed to the disciples (instead of to Jesus): they hear the divine approbation of Jesus as the messianic Son. Suddenly, Elijah and Moses had disappeared and Jesus stood alone. "Listen to him" – the Beloved Son is also the prophet-like-Moses (Dt 18:15-19) whose teaching must be heeded.

Mark intends us to see in the transfigured Jesus an anticipated glimpse of the risen Lord. As such, the episode is representative of that stage of christology which looked upon the resurrection as the decisive christological moment (see Rom 1:3-4; Acts 2:32-36; 5:30-31; 13:32-33). Jesus was not a mere equal of Moses and Elijah. He was supremely greater than they because by his victory over death he had been designated Son of God in power. Yet again, through the technique of Peter's misunderstanding, Mark has corrected a christological error of some in his church (see 8:31-33). He can now resume his narrative. All was normal again. The disciples saw before them, quite alone, their Master, no longer transformed but in his familiar guise of every day.

The disciples had glimpsed the glory of Jesus; they would not understand "until the Son of Man had risen from the dead" (9:9). Not until then could he be proclaimed with understanding and in truth. Typically, the disciples had not grasped the teaching, not even what "resurrection" meant (v 10). Their problem was: how could Jesus be raised from the dead before and apart from the general resurrection at the end? It is a signal to the Christian; he or she must strive to grasp the mighty, transforming import of the resurrection. It is promise of life beyond the seeming finality of death.

The Elijah-passage (9:11-13) is an answer to a difficulty that faced the early church. Christians believed that Jesus was the Messiah. But Jewish tradition, based on Malachi 3:2-5; 4:5-6, held that Elijah's return would precede "the great and terrible day of the Lord." Implied in Mark's text (9:11) is a denial that Elijah had come. Jesus answered that the tradition about Elijah was based on Scripture. The second part of the reply (9:12b-13) faced up to another objection: the Christian claim that John the Baptist was the promised Elijah-figure was disproved by the well-known fate of the Baptist. The reply is in terms of Baptist-Jesus typology. The baptist's fate was prophetic of the fate of the Messiah. "As it is written of him" – see 1 Kings 19:2,10 – John "had found his Jezebel in Herodias" (see Mk 6:17-28). It was fitting that the precursor should, beforehand, walk the way the Son of Man must walk – a point made explicitly in Mt 17:12. The Christian retort to the Jewish objection was that John was the perfect Elijah to the Messiah who had come.

Galilee (Mk 14:28; 16:7)

"But after I am raised up, I will go before you to Galilee" (14:28). "But go, tell his disciples and Peter that he is going ahead of you to Galilee; there you will see him" (16:7).

In Mark 16:7 the women were given a message, the echo of a promise made by Jesus on the way to Gethsemane (14:28), a message for the disciples and especially for Peter (that is the force of the Greek). Jesus was going before them into Galilee; they will see him there. Mark's "Galilee" is not a precise region on a map but is the area of Gentile mission. Mark has been at pains to show the wider "Galilee" as the place where crowds gathered from all of ancient Israel (3:7-8) and as the locale of the breakdown of the barrier between Jew and Gentile (7:31). There the disciples had been first assembled (1:16-20) and there they will now "see": they will encounter the risen Christ (16:7). Meanwhile, life goes on in the darkness of faith because Jesus is not yet fully revealed. The cross still casts its shadow and life is real and earnest (13:9-13). But the consummation is sure and will be as fully a reality as the former ministry in Galilee. The cross was not the end. It was the birthpangs of a new life of the good news. The promise of Jesus in Mk 14:28 is not too far removed from the commission of the Lord in Mt 18:19 – "Go therefore and make disciples of all nations ..."

KING

The charge that led to the crucifixion was the claim that Jesus was "king of the Jews" – "Pilate asked him, 'Are you the King of the Jews?' He answered him, 'You say so.'" By the high priest Jesus had been asked, in Jewish terms, if he were the Messiah, the Son of the Blessed (14:61). The Roman uses a title that has meaning for him: King of the Jews. In his estimation the title was political and, if Jesus really claimed it, was equivalent to high treason: political authority was Rome's prerogative. Pilate's question falls into a pattern wherein a title is bestowed which is true of Jesus but not in the sense of those who bestow it (3:11; 8:29; 14:61; 15:2). That is why Jesus' response ("You say so") is evasive. In fact, he does accept the designation, but knows that he is King of a kind not imagined by Pilate. John has a splendid commentary on this exchange (Jn 18:33-37). In Mark's eyes, the title is certainly important and he has highlighted it by means of his bracket technique – "Pilate asked him" (15:2, "Pilate asked him again" (15:4). From now on, in the passion narrative, the title appears at every conceivable opportunity. The title also indicates that the strategy of Jesus' priestly opponents was to show him linked with a political-messianic movement and to have him condemned as a revolutionary.

Barabbas (15:6-15)

The Jewish crowd came to plead for Barabbas and Pilate presented them with an alternative: they may have instead "the King of the Jews" (15:8-9). He has seen through the charges made against Jesus. Mark put the responsibility where he believed it belonged, at the door of the priests (v 11). As in all the gospels, Pilate was convinced of Jesus' innocence, but yielded to pressure. Pilate's strange appeal to the crowd (v 12) as to what he is to do with this King of the Jews is, dramatically, very effective. The nation rejected its king and called for his death on a cross. Pilate helplessly protested Jesus' innocence – "Why, what evil has he done?" – but they clamoured for blood. Pilate yielded, "wishing to satisfy the crowd." Pilate "handed him over" – "delivered him" – (v 15): he had played his role in a drama directed by God.

Mockery (15:6-32)

Into the narrative of the sentencing and execution of Jesus (15:6-15; 21-32), Mark has inserted the incident of mocking by soldiers (vv 16-20), thereby highlighting the title "King of the Jews." This brutal mockery was, ironically, Jesus' enthronement. The soldiers led him inside the palace, the Roman procurator's headquarters in Jerusalem. The "whole batallion" means, most likely, those who were about at the time. But the statement does add to the mock solemnity of the situation: this "King" had his palace guards. The "purple cloak" was, very likely, one of the red-coloured military cloaks; the "crown" (rather, "diadem") was a rude replica hastily woven of thorns. A "purple" cloak and a "crown" of thorns furnished a mock ritual of royal acclaim. The soldiers' salutation, based on the charge on which Jesus was condemned (see 15:2,9,12) is a parody of the greeting to the Roman emperor: *Ave Caesar, victor, imperator*. Striking and spitting seem out of place and most likely come from the other mocking scene in 14:65. Here the emphasis is on royal "homage." The irony of the situation is patent and admirably suits Mark's christology. Jesus is King – but in humility (11:7-10) and suffering. Now he can be conducted to his throne: the cross. "And the inscription of the charge against him read, 'The King of the Jews.'" The King was enthroned and proclaimed. See Jn 19:19-22.

SON OF MAN

"The Son of Man" occurs more than eighty times in the gospels and, practically without exception, as a self-designation by Jesus. Jesus, however, never set out the meaning of the phrase; nor was it ever used to identify him. In gospel usage it had become a title of Jesus. The expression itself is Semitic – a literal rendering of Aramaic idiom. The background of the title is, ultimately, Daniel 7. There, in an apocalyptic setting, one "like a son of man" (a human being) came into the presence of God and was granted dominion and kingship (Dan 7:13-14). In Daniel this figure was a heavenly counterpart of "the holy ones of the Most High" (7:27), the faithful Jews resisting unto death the persecution of Antiochus IV (the Maccabean era). In later apocalyptic Jewish circles this image of a heavenly Son of Man was further developed. A case can be made that, in first century AD Jewish apocalyptic circles, a picture had emerged of a messianic figure of heavenly origin who had authority from God. This may well have entered into Jesus' understanding of his mission. Nevertheless, it has been doubted that Jesus could have referred to himself as "the Son of Man." At most, it is maintained, he may have used "son of man" in a neutral sense to refer to himself indirectly. At first sight quite plausible, this view is, on closer scrutiny, seen to lack a sustainable base.

There is the distinct possibility that Jesus, reflecting on Daniel 7 and other Old Testament passages, had seized on that "one like a son of man" to whom God had given glory and dominion and had interpreted it as "the Son of Man," the specific human figure through whom God manifests his victory. He would have seen himself as this instrument of God's plan. R.E. Brown observes, pertinently: "A Jesus who did not reflect on the Old Testament and use the interpretative techniques of his time is an unrealistic projection who surely never existed."[21] Early Christians embraced the title, extended its use, and acknowledged it as a self-designation of Jesus. There are three types of Son of Man sayings in the gospels:

1. Those which refer to the earthly activity of the Son of Man.
2. Those which refer to the suffering of the Son of Man.
3. Those which refer to the future glory and *parousia* of the Son of Man.

Two occurrences of the title in Mark refer to the earthly activity of the Son of Man (Mk 2:10, 28). In the passage 2:1-12, the evangelist tells us that the cure of the paralytic was intended to manifest the sin-forgiving power of the Son of Man: "So that you may know that the Son of Man has authority on earth to forgive sins" (2:10). In the early kerygma, remission of sins was regarded as intrinsic to the experience of being Christian. Thus Acts 10:43 states, "All the prophets testify about him (Jesus) that everyone who believes in him receives forgiveness of sins through his name." In the light of this and similar texts it is evident that early Christians proclaimed the forgiveness of sin as a present fact. This meant a head-on clash with Jewish belief which regarded forgiveness as a hoped-for future benefit.

The emergence of the forgiveness of sins debate in the gospel is an indication that it was a live issue in Mark's community. Their assertion of forgiveness of sins on earth, an assertion made in the name of Jesus, was blasphemy to their Jewish adversaries – "Who can forgive sins but God alone?" (2:7). Their defence was in their claim of a share in the authority of the eschatological Son of Man (v 10). For Mark the full revelation of the Son of Man was in his suffering, death and resurrection and so was accessible only to believers. When, however, those who believe in Jesus seek to live and act in the Spirit of Jesus, they participated in his power to forgive sins. The story of 2:1-12 became a vindication of the Church's claim to declare forgiveness of sins in the name of Jesus (see Jn 20:23), a forgiveness achieved in baptism.

Though it appears as a sabbath controversy, the passage 2:23-26 does not directly regard the problem of the sabbath. The focus is on the significance of an incident in David's flight from Saul (1 Sam 21:1-6). He and his men had come to the sanctuary of Nob where the priest Ahimelech, aware of their need, gave them the consecrated loaves, reserved for the priests: in case of need law has to yield to human concern. In Mark the essential factor remains the comparison between David and Jesus. The interest is christological: Jesus, as God's anointed one, has the same freedom as David in respect of the law. Mark developed his christological thrust in v 28 (see 2:10) in the light of 2:23-27: "so the Son of Man is Lord even of the sabbath." The matter was of importance because sabbath observance was a lively issue in the early church (see Lk 14:10-17; Jn 5:1-19; 9:1-11). At an early stage Christians began to observe not the Jewish sabbath but the day of resurrection, "the Lord's day" (Rev 1:10); this, of course, brought them into conflict with Judaism. They maintained that their Lord had set the sabbath free and their distinctive observance was traced back to his authority. The Marcan Jesus had claimed God-given authority to define the true meaning of the sabbath: "The sabbath was made for humankind, and not humankind for the sabbath" (v 27). Decoded, this reads: Religion is for men and women, not men and women for religion. He had defined the true meaning of religion – it is for men and women.

Suffering Son of God

Apart from 2:10, 28 all Son of Man sayings are in the second half of Mark's gospel and, predominantly, regard the suffering of the Son of Man. This is explicit in the first of these occurrences: "The Son of Man must undergo great suffering" (8:31). "Must" *(dei)* expresses a conviction that the sufferings of the Messiah fall within a divine purpose, a purpose discernible in scripture, the word of God (see 9:12). Luke (24:26-27) states clearly: "Was it not necessary *(edei)* that the Messiah should suffer these things and then enter his glory? ... He interpreted to them the things about himself in all the scriptures." Mark 8:31 is the first of three predictions of the passion. The second prediction, "The Son of Man is to be betrayed [delivered up] into human hands" (9:31), is likely to be close to the original form of the basic passion-prediction. The third prediction, 10:33-34, the most detailed of the three, is, most obviously, *a vaticinium ex eventu*; it is, in effect, a mini passion narrative.

At the transfiguration episode, the three disciples (Peter, James, John) had glimpsed the anticipated glory of Jesus. They were bound to silence "until after the Son of Man had risen from the dead" (9:9). The transfiguration had manifested the Son of God; the privileged disciples were charged not to divulge the secret. The disciples would not understand the mystery of his suffering and glory until the crucified Jesus will have risen from the dead. Not until then can he be proclaimed with understanding and in truth. Like the reference to resurrection at the close of each of the three predictions, this too went over the heads of the disciples. The Christian is reminded that the risen Christ is to be understood in the light of the cross and suffering. And the note of suffering is again struck without delay: "How then is it written of the Son of Man, that he is to go through many sufferings and be treated with contempt?" (9:12). The context was a question about Elijah, popularly expected to precede the Messiah. The answer, in short, as we have seen above, was that a Baptist who suffered a violent death was the fitting Elijah to a suffering Son of Man.

In Gethsemane the same three disciples could not hear Jesus' word of warning because "their eyes were very heavy" (14:40). They had closed their eyes to what had transpired at Gethsemane. Their chronic misunderstanding (a distinctive feature of Mark's narrative) had grown into failure; Peter had reverted to being Simon again (v 37). The last suffering Son of Man saying fell on deaf ears: "The hour has come; the Son of Man is betrayed [delivered up] into the hands of sinners" (14:41). The three passion predictions were about to be fulfilled. And there is the challenge to disciples. The ground of the paradoxical behaviour required of disciples – that the first must be "slave" of all (10:42-44) – is to be found in the example of the Son of Man: "For the Son of Man came not to be served but to serve, and to give his life a ransom for many" (10:45). The saying specified in what sense Jesus was to "serve" people: he would give his life as a "ransom" for them. *Lytron* ("ransom") was originally a commercial term: ransom was the price to be paid to redeem a pledge, to recover a pawned object, or to free a slave. In the Septuagint, the term is predicated metaphorically of God who was frequently said to have bought, acquired, purchased, ransomed, his people (see Ps 49:8; Is 63:4). In its Marcan form the saying is related to Is 53:10-11 and "ransom" is to be understood in the sense of the Hebrew word *asham* of Is 53:10, "an offering for sin," an atonement offering. By laying down his life for a humankind enslaved to sin, Jesus fulfilled the saying about the Servant in Is 53:10-11. Jesus had paid the universal debt: he had given his life to redeem all others. But this is metaphor, not crude commerce. The death of Jesus, in the Father's purpose and in the Son's acceptance, was a gesture of sheer love. Any suggestion that the death of the Son was, in any sense at all, literal payment of a debt, the placating of an offended God, is blasphemy. God is ever motivated by love, not "justice."

However shattering the betrayal by Judas (14:17-21) it was in accordance with a divine purpose in the unrolling of the passion – "as it is written." "For the Son of Man goes as it is written of him, but woe to that one by whom the Son of Man is betrayed [delivered up]" (v 21). What is written is that the Son of Man "goes": death was freely accepted by Jesus himself. And, behind it all, is a chastening admonition to the reader. Mark has placed the betrayal episode in the setting of eucharistic table fellowship. The Christian must ask, "Is it I?" – am I a betrayer of the Lord Jesus? One is reminded of Paul in 1 Cor 11:28 – "Examine yourselves, and only then eat of the bread and drink of the cup."

The Glory of the Son of Man

The passage Mark 8:34-38, coming directly after the first passion prediction (8:31-33), asserts, unequivocally, that the disciples of this Son of Man must necessarily walk in his path. V 34 had shown the condition of discipleship and thereby had sketched a portrait of the loyal disciple: one who is committed to the following of Jesus, one who is not ashamed of that following. Now we are shown the contrast: one who will not follow, one who is ashamed of Jesus and of his way of humiliation and suffering (v 38). A warning sounds for such a one: the Son of Man, too, will be ashamed of such a one, will disown that person, when he returns in glory at the end of time (v 38). Just as the disciples should not have been ashamed of the earthly Jesus, Christians must not be ashamed of the word of the Lord whom they encounter in the proclamation. This solemn pronouncement – "of them the Son of Man will be ashamed when he comes in the glory of his Father" – was of major importance for the Marcan community. But it is a word of warning, not a judgment saying. The Son of Man will not come to execute judgment but to gather his elect (13:17). The warning is that one may not be recognizable as belonging to Christ.

Parousia

In the farewell discourse (ch 13), after a warning of "tribulation" (vv 9-13), comes the triumph of the Son of Man (13:24-27). Mark certainly believed in a parousia (advent) of the Son of Man and was convinced that it was imminent; in this he showed the common expectation of early Christians. The passage vv 24-27 is a collage of prophetic texts. The cosmic signs which are to accompany the parousia (vv 24-25) were part and parcel of Jewish apocalyptic descriptions of the Day of the Lord. The parousia marks the definitive manifestation of the Son of Man: "Then they will see the Son of Man coming in clouds with great power and glory" (v 26). The Son of Man will be seen: seen in fulness instead of being dimly perceived. This is the real message of hope for Christians. This promise and this hope they cling to while the Lord is absent (2:20; 13:34). It is this that enables them, no matter what their present situation (13:9-13) to endure to the end. Already 8:38 had warned that only those who, here and now, in this vale of tears, were not "ashamed" of a suffering Son of Man would rejoice in his glorious coming. That is why Mark went on, insistently, to urge watching and readiness for the coming (vv 33-37). And, for the faithful ones, the coming will be joy indeed. The Son of Man will not come to execute judgment. The sole purpose of his appearing will be to gather his elect (13:27). After his consoling presentation of the parousia, Mark developed that encouragement by stressing the nearness of the coming (vv 28-30). He insisted that the intervening time be spent in watchfulness. True to his understanding of discipleship, outlined in chapters 8-10, he maintained that there could be no room for complacency in the life of the Christian.

"I am."

The silence of Jesus (14:61) in face of the high priest's challenge that he respond to the charges of the witnesses (14:56-59), a silence carefully underlined ("but he was silent and did not answer", v 61), is dramatic preparation for the solemn confession of v 62. The high priest was forced to take direct action; his question and Jesus' answer form the heart of this passage (14:53-65). Thoroughly Marcan, these verses are a high point of his christology. The titles "Christ" and "Son of God" stand in the heading of the gospel (1:1). The high priest now ironically bestowed them on Jesus (Son of the Blessed is equivalently Son of God). When Jesus was acknowledged as Messiah at Caesarea Philippi he enjoined silence (8:30). But now Jesus himself, positively and publicly, acknowledged that he is the Messiah, and that he is indeed the Son of God. He did so on his own terms, in terms of "Son of Man". With his firm "I am" he made, for the first and only time, an explicit messianic claim. He could do so because now there was no risk of triumphalist misinterpretation: he was manifestly a suffering Messiah (see 8:31). Use of "the Blessed One" and "the Power," though not really precise Jewish terminology, did, for Mark, provide a "Jewish" colouring. His "you will see" refers to the Christian perception of Jesus "at the right hand of God" by resurrection and "coming with the clouds of heaven" at the parousia.

SON OF GOD

The New Testament church confessed Jesus as Son of God – and, in doing so, attributed to Jesus a unique relationship to God. The question, then, is: was the title Son of God bestowed on Jesus during his lifetime? The title was used, in association with Messiah, by the high priest (14:61) – but the passage between the high priest and Jesus (14:61-62) reflects the christology of the evangelist. The heavenly voice, at baptism and transfiguration, declaring Jesus to be "my Son, the Beloved" (1:11; 9:7) is for the sake of the readers. The confession of the centurion (15:39) at that moment in the gospel is a firm christological statement. Ironically, the one text in which Jesus referred to himself absolutely as the Son ("about that day or hour no one knows, neither the angels in heaven, nor the Son, but only the Father," 13:32) implies his subordination to the Father. On the other hand, Jesus did address God in Aramaic as *Abba* (14:36). There is no evidence that, in Palestinian Judaism, *abba* was used in address to God. Jesus' usage is distinctive and suggests his consciousness of a unique relationship.

The Secret

It was firmly Mark's view (his so-called "messianic secret") that no human being could acknowledge in faith and truth that Jesus is the Son of God before the paradoxical revelation of his identity through his death on the cross. The divine voice, at baptism and transfiguration, did proclaim Jesus' Sonship. The demons also, with preternatural insight, could perceive what neither people nor disciples discerned: the true nature of Jesus. The unclean spirits become guides to the reader! Their being bound to silence is a reminder that, to know and proclaim the truth, one must, like the centurion, come to terms with the cross (15:39).

The celebrated designation "Messianic Secret" is a misnomer. The element of secrecy concerns not Jesus' messiahship but his identity as Son of God. It follows that the titles "Messiah," "King," "Son of Man," are not, in the evangelist's estimation, wholly adequate. Mark takes care to identify his own evaluative point of view with that of the protagonist of his story: Jesus. Consequently, there is only one correct way in which to view things: the way of Jesus, which is also Mark's own way. The evangelist took a step further and made certain that both his assessment and that of Jesus were in accord with the point of view of God. It follows that the perception of Jesus which is normative in Mark's story is God's perception. If this is so, then the title which God bestowed on Jesus is of paramount importance.

The heading of the gospel – "The beginning of the good news of Jesus Christ, the Son of God" (1:1) – informs the reader of Mark's own understanding of Jesus' identity. In the baptismal scene the heavenly voice (the voice of God) declared of Jesus: "You are my Son, the Beloved" (1:11). As Jesus was about to embark on his public ministry, God solemnly affirmed both his status and his call. Similarly, at the transfiguration, God declared (this time for the benefit of the three disciples): "This is my Son, the Beloved; listen to him!" (9:7). Only at baptism and transfiguration does God emerge as "actor" in the story. And not alone did God, each time, declare that Jesus was "Son", but the declaration served the purpose of confirmation. The baptism declaration confirmed the truth of the caption (1:1); the transfiguration declaration confirmed the truth of Peter's confession of Jesus as the "Messiah" (8:29).

Since this is so, the "Son of Man" of 8:29 is not meant to be a corrective of "Messiah" of 8:29, no more than is "Son of Man" of 14:62 corrective of "Messiah, the Son of the Blessed One" of 14:61. What is so is that Peter's Caesarea Philippi confession, though correct, is "insufficient" because, as Peter understood it, it did justice neither to the identity nor to the mission of Jesus. At the trial, Jesus' "I am" (14:62) acknowledged the truth of God's point of view regarding him. The high priest showed himself to be one of "those outside" (4:11) because he did not believe the truth of the claim and was seeking to entrap Jesus. Finally, at the climactic moment of the death of Jesus the title was Son of God: "Truly, this man was God's Son!" (15:39). This centurion was the first human being in Mark's story to penetrate the secret of Jesus' identity, because he was the first to come to terms with the cross.

As for the meaning of "Son of God" – the voice from heaven is a composite quotation: from Ps 2:7; Is 42:1; Gen 22:2. In Is 42:1 the servant in whom God delights is one "chosen" for ministry; in Gen 22:2 Abraham's beloved son is his "only" son. Most importantly, in Ps 2:7, "you are my son" is declared by Yahweh of the Davidic king. Consequently, God solemnly affirms that "Jesus, the Anointed One (Messiah-King) from the line of David, is his only or unique Son whom he has chosen for eschatological ministry."[22]

CONCLUSION

Mark's Christians were followers of Jesus, who believed that he is Christ and Son of God. Yet, they had much to learn. The evangelist set out to declare who Jesus is, to spell out the nature of his Messiahship. It is easy enough, he realises, to declare, even with conviction: You are the Messiah. What matters is how one understands that confession. It does not ask too much of one to be a willing disciple of a risen Lord. We, all of us, find triumph and glory congenial. Mark takes an uncompromising stand. Jesus is, of course, Messiah and Son of God; he is the one who will, without, fail, come to gather his elect. But he is, too, the suffering Son of Man, who walked a lone path to his death, who died, as it seemed to him, abandoned even by God. Mark stresses that only one who has come to terms with the cross can understand the resurrection of the Lord. Jesus was one who was glorified because he had accepted the *kenósis*, the self-abasement, of his life and death. That is why Jesus was, for the first time, formally acknowledged by a human as Son of God as he hung lifeless on the tree (15:39)

Jesus is Messiah, of that Mark was sure – but he is a disconcerting Messiah. The question stands, writ large: Who, then, is this? That Jesus would have permitted himself to be taken by his enemies, to be maltreated and mocked by them, and put to death, is something that the contemporaries of Jesus and the readers of Mark could hardly comprehend. Yet, if one has not come to terms with this "scandal," one has not grasped the originality of Jesus, in particular, the Jesus portrayed by Mark. Jesus did not come as judge with sentence and punishment for those who would not receive the gift of forgiveness and salvation he offered to them. He had come as the one who would let himself be crushed by the evil intent of whose who resisted him and would be rid of him.

At first sight, a suffering Son of Man, painfully vulnerable, and a Son of Man radiant in divine glory, seem contradictory. In actual terms of the Jesus story there is no contradiction. In Luke, the message was spelled out for the Emmaus disciples: "Was it not necessary that the Messiah should suffer these things and then enter into his glory?" (Lk 24:26). For Jesus, glory followed on suffering. It is the insight of the John of Revelation: the Victim is the Victor. Glory beyond suffering is a concrete expression of the truth that *exousia* ("power", "authority") is most authentically present in *diakonia* ("service"). This is borne out by the two "earthly" Son of Man sayings: the Son of Man with authority to forgive sins and the Son of Man, Lord of the sabbath. Here is where, with urgency, the Son of Man is to be sought and found. Jesus, friend of sinners, mirrors a God of forgiveness. Jesus put people before observance. It was precisely because of his commitment to people, precisely because he was perceived as friend of sinners, that Jesus suffered the torture of the cross. It was precisely because of his commitment that God exalted him. When *exousia* is not *diakonia*, when forgiveness is not prodigal, the Son of Man is not being represented. The suffering Son of Man, rejected friend of sinners, must be embraced and confessed before any who claim to be his disciples can proclaim the Son of Man of glory. Mark is wholly consistent.

In the long run, what is incomprehensible is the rejection and death of the promised Messiah who would establish the rule of God, of the Son of God who would reveal the Father. The originality of Jesus flows from the contrast between his heavenly authority and power, and the humiliation of his crucifixion. Mark's "messianic secret" is designed to reconcile two theological affirmations: Jesus, from the first, was indeed Messiah and yet had to receive from the Father, through the abasement of the cross, his title of Messiah. The meaning of his life is that as Son of God sent by the Father, he had come to deliver men and women from all their enemies, from foes within and foes without. He came to forgive sins, not to chastise sinners. He came, but he will not impose. When it came to the test, rather than force the human heart, he humbled himself and permitted himself to be taken and shamed and put to death.

CHAPTER 8

The Cross

We proclaim Christ crucified, a stumbling block to Jews and foolishness to Gentiles, but to those who are called, both Jews and Greeks, Christ the power of God and the wisdom of God. (1 Cor 1:23).

Mark's gospel is a *theologia crucis* – a theology of the cross. Understandably, this concern comes to a head in his passion narrative. It is evident in the Gethsemane episode (14:32-44) – "he began to be distressed and agitated" (v 33): Jesus is shattered. He died with an anguished shout: "My God, my God, why have you forsaken me?" (15:34). Mark has Jesus die in total isolation, without any relieving feature at all. It is only after death that Jesus is clearly recognized and acknowledged by any human in the awed confession of the centurion: "Truly, this man was God's Son!" (15:39). Mark is making a theological point: salvation is never of oneself, not even for Jesus. That awful and awesome journey to the cross is comfort for all who have seen in Jesus of Nazareth the image of the invisible God. It is the consolation of all who have found in him the ultimate assurance that God is on our side. It is, above all, comfort to all who find it hard to bear the cross. It was not easy for the Master.

Prophecy of failure (Mk 14:26-31)

On the way to the Mount of Olives Jesus spoke forebodingly of the fate of his disciples. He quoted Zechariah 13:7 to the effect that since Jesus the caring shepherd will be struck down, his defenceless sheep will be scattered. He then promised, in a reversal of the scattering, that after his resurrection he will be again their shepherd in Galilee; the flock will be reconstituted (see 16:7). Peter, who had earlier challenged Jesus (8:27-34) now again challenges him (14:29).

Mark, like the other evangelists, has Jesus predicting Peter's three-fold denial. Peter vehemently rebutted the warning and the others echoed his avowal of readiness to die with Jesus. The reader knows that the Twelve will fail, abysmally; but Jesus will not abandon them. Mark is holding out hope to Christians who may fail.

Gethsemane (14:32-42)

We had not long to wait for discipleship failure. All of them had heard his predictions of suffering and death; Peter, James and John had heard the heavenly voice (9:7); James and John had confidently declared their readiness to share his cup (10:38-39). Now, at Geth-semane, he took the three to be with him in his hour of need – they do not act as disciples. At Gethsemane Jesus asked his "disciples" to pray – they will not act as disciples. Jesus himself went apart to pray; he realised that he was on his own. Mark's Gethsemane-scene shows that Jesus did not fully understand God's way, shows that he did not want to die. While we can plausibly assert that *Abba* was Jesus' preferred address to his God, the word *abba* occurs only once in the gospels – here in Mk 14:36. There is a fittingness to its appear-ance here: the familiar title seems to be wrested from Jesus at this awful moment. He prayed, explicitly, that the cup be taken from him. He did not contemplate suffering and a horrible death with stoical calm. He was appalled at the prospect. He knew fear. He was brave as he rose above his dread to embrace what his God asked. But he must know if the path which opened before him was indeed the way that God would have him walk. He found assur-ance in prayer: the utterance of his trustful "Abba" already included "thy will be done." His decision was to trust God despite the dark-ness of his situation. His prayer did not go unanswered – though the answer was paradoxical. As the letter to the Hebrews puts it: "he was heard because of his reverent submission" (5:7). The obedi-ent Son cried out to the Father and put himself wholly in the hands of the Father.

If Jesus said of the disciples, "the spirit indeed is willing, but the flesh is weak," that statement is not irrelevant to his own situation. Jesus himself had experienced human vulnerability: distress, agita-tion, and grief even to the point of death, to the point of asking the Father that the hour might pass him by and the cup be taken away. "Hour" and "cup" indicate the historical moment and the immin-ent prospect of appalling death. But this, too, was the eschatological hour of the final struggle, the great *peirasmos*, "trial," before the triumph of God's kingdom. "The Son of Man is given over to the hands of sinners" (14:41). In the Old Testament God gives over the wicked to punishment; here, in contrast, a just man is "given over" by God. At the end Jesus invited his disciples: "Get up, let us be going." Jesus still includes his disciples, even though they had failed him.

It is important that Mark has so closely woven the theme of disciple misunderstanding with that of Jesus' testing. It is his most dramatic answer to any objection to a suffering Messiah. Jesus himself had been brought to the brink of rejecting it. The evangelist leaves no doubt that suffering messiahship is not easily accepted; he knows, as fully as Paul, that the cross is foolishness and scandal. The three disciples did not understand. The reader is duly warned. One must watch and pray. Good intentions are not enough. Discipleship is a way of life. And the course of that way has been plotted by Jesus: "Get up, let us be going ..."

The arrest (14:43-52)

Jesus was ready and the drama opened without delay. The Son of Man went to his fate in obedience to a divine purpose (see 14:21). His lot was indeed bitter: "one of the twelve" was hastening to betray him. Judas was accompanied by an armed rabble, one dispatched by the religious authorities; their plot was bearing fruit (14:1-2). There is no mention of temple police (Lk 22:52) or Roman troops (Jn 18:3,12). The "betrayer" is, literally, "the one who delivered him up" – Judas is serving a divine purpose. Judas greeted Jesus in the manner in which a disciple would salute his rabbi; yet betrayal with a kiss is singularly distasteful and Luke underlines the fact (Lk 22:48). In the Marcan narrative Jesus did not speak to Judas. The person who wounded the high priest's slave is not named, in contrast to John 18:10 where the wielder of the sword is Peter and the slave is named Malchus; while Luke notes that Jesus healed the wound. Mark gives the impression of a clumsy attempt to defend Jesus by someone other than a disciple. Jesus protested at the manner of the arrest: it characterized him as a man of violence. But he was a man of peace, a teacher who did not need to disguise his teaching. The phrase "day by day in the temple" implies a longer

Jerusalem ministry than the few days allowed by Mark. Reference to the fulfillment of the scriptures does not point to specific texts but asserts that here God's will is being done: the Son of Man is being delivered up. The "all" who fled are the disciples. They forsook him. Even one who still "followed" Jesus after the disciples had deserted quickly lost heart. Jesus was left all alone. Traditionally, the "young man" of vv 51-52 has been taken to be the evangelist. Rather, it would seem that, for Mark, this was a would-be disciple. His shameful flight dramatized disciple failure and carried its message for later disciples who may have failed. Ultimately it is a message of hope because of the promise of restoration (14:28; 16:7).

Before the Jewish authorities (14:53-15:1)

The opening verse (14:53) makes two affirmations: the leading away of Jesus and the assembling of priests, elders and scribes. Mark has built on the tradition that Jesus was brought before the Jewish high priest (see Lk 22:54; Jn 18:13). Peter is introduced – he had followed Jesus "at a distance." It will shortly emerge how very far behind he is on the way of discipleship. Jesus' testimony is framed by Peter's denials. He was faithful unto death, while Peter proved unfaithful. At Caesarea Philippi Peter showed that he could not accept the notion of suffering messiahship (8:31-33). Now he would disassociate himself from the suffering Messiah. But first the trial of Jesus got underway.

The opening remark (v 55) harks back to 3:6; 11:18; 12:12 and 14:1 – Jesus had long been tried and condemned. All that remained was how to make away with him. His enemies needed evidence. And the witnesses were there. The influence of the psalms is manifest: "for false witnesses have risen against me, and they are breathing out violence" (Ps 27:12); "Malicious witnesses rise up" (Ps 35:11). Mark stresses their lack of agreement. The repetition of the lack of agreement (v 56b "and their testimony did not agree," v 59 "But even on this point their testimony did not agree") is the frame for a Marcan insertion: "We heard him say, 'I will destroy this temple that is made with hands, and in three days I will build another, not made with hands'" (14:56). He thus signals the special importance of the saying.

Mark emphasises the falsity of the testimony. Yet, there is wide attestation that Jesus had spoken against the Temple (see Mt 26:61; Jn 2:19; Acts 6:14). Besides, the cursing of the fig tree episode does present Jesus as "destroying the temple:" "the fig tree that you cursed has withered" (Mk 11:21). He did claim to have brought the Temple to an end: that is the point of the mocking repetition of the charge as he hung on the cross (15:29). Ironically, the taunt was true, symbolically demonstrated by the rending of the temple veil (15:38). The temple had lost its meaning for Christians. And this was because Jesus had built another temple "not made with hands" – the community. This was his purpose in calling and forming disciples. John offers a different explanation: Jesus spoke of the temple of his body (Jn 2:21).

It suits Mark's purpose that the testimony of these witnesses cannot be the decisive factor in Jesus' trial. That must be the formal messianic claim of Jesus himself (v 62). When pressed by the high priest to respond to the charges, Jesus maintained a rigid silence (vv 60-61a). The silence of Jesus, carefully emphasized ("but he was silent and did not answer," v 61) is dramatic preparation for the solemn confession of v 62. The high priest was forced to take direct action; his question and Jesus' answer form the heart of this passage. Thoroughly Marcan, these verses are the culmination of his christology. The titles "Christ" and "Son of God" stand in the heading of the gospel (1:1). The high priest now ironically bestowed them on Jesus (Son of the Blessed is the equivalent of Son of God). When Jesus was acknowledged as Christ at Caesarea Philippi he enjoined silence (8:30). But now Jesus himself, positively and publicly, acknowledged that he is the Messiah, and that he is indeed Son of God. But he did so on his own terms, in terms of "Son of Man." With his firm "I am" he made, for the first and only time, an explicit messianic claim. He could do so because now there was no risk of triumphalist misinterpretation: he was manifestly a suffering Messiah (see 8:31). Mark's use of "the Blessed One" and "the Power," though not really precise Jewish terminology, do, for Mark, provide a "Jewish" colouring. His "you will see" refers to the Christian perception of Jesus "at the right hand of God" by resurrection and "coming with the clouds of heaven" at the *parousia*.

Jesus' confession provoked the death-sentence and that is how it had to be because he cannot be known for who he is until he has died and risen from the dead (see 9:9). In terms of the trial-narrative, his claim was self-incriminating. The Sanhedrin can now achieve its stated purpose (v 55). The rending of garments had become, in the case of the high priest, a carefully regulated formal judicial gesture. Only Mark (followed by Matthew) specifies a charge of blasphemy. It reflects the situation of the early church: Jewish authorities had begun to regard the Christian claims for Jesus as blasphemous. And Christians would have suffered for their confession of him (see 13:9-11). It is not unlikely, however, that Jesus, in the estimation of the Sanhedrin, was a false prophet – one who had made blasphemous claims; he had arrogated to himself divine prerogatives (such as forgiveness of sin).

The mocking episode (v 65) appears to be a separate element of tradition introduced by Mark at this point. The "some" implies members of the Sanhedrin. That Mark intends the implication is evident when we note that he has made them explicitly mock Jesus on the cross (15:31). Historically unlikely, it is fitting in Mark's narrative. The leaders had sought his death from 3:6 and now triumph has its hour. The irony of this scene is that Jesus is being mocked as a prophet just as his prediction of Peter's denial is being fulfilled.

Peter's denials (14:66-72)

With v 66 we return to Peter. In the setting and form of the denials, Mark is on traditional grounds. His title for Jesus, however, is "Nazarene" (see 1:24; 10:47; 14:57; 16:1), indicative of his interest in Galilee. At the initial stage Peter was evasive, pretending not to understand what the maid was saying (v 68). On the basis of this first (traditional) denial Mark has built the other two, so producing his familiar triadic pattern. Peter had to come out and deny that he was "one of them," a disciple of Jesus (v 70). Finally, he was forced to disassociate himself from Jesus, calling down the wrath of God upon himself if what he says is not true (v 71). The progression is patent: evasion, denial of discipleship, denial under oath that he had known Jesus at all. The cockcrow – Mark alone mentions that the cock crowed a second time – caused Peter to remember Jesus' prediction of his denials and his own vehement protestation (14:30-31). "He broke down" – an approximate translation of an enigmatic verb, but the general idea is clear enough: Peter was utterly shattered. The denial-story brings the disciple-misunderstanding theme (prominent throughout the gospel) to a head. Peter had publicly disassociated himself from Jesus. The sheep had been effectively scattered and the stricken shepherd was wholly on his own (see 14:27). As they see themselves in disciples who could betray and deny and forsake, Mark's readers are not likely to feel complacent. Mark insists on the loneliness of Jesus during his passion: up to the moment of death he is alone, more and more alone. His intention is not only to awaken us to the poignancy of this painful solitude. He wants us to perceive in that starkness the truth that God alone saves.

In the story of Peter's denials Mark may well have had Christian experience in view. Persecution could be, and was, sharp and painful. Not all could bear up with what must have been heroic courage. What then?

> Was all hope lost for those who failed and denied Christ? A Peter who had once denied and later borne witness could constitute an encouragement that repentance and a second chance were possible. For that reason it may have been important to underline the seriousness of what Peter had done. Before his arrest Jesus had warned his disciples, 'Keep on praying lest you enter into trial/testing/temptation [*peirasmos*]" precisely because they were not yet sufficiently strong. But with bravado, Peter by attempting to follow had entered into *peirasmos* and failed.[23]

Before Pilate (15:1-15)

Mark picks up the thread of the story which had been interrupted by the account of Peter's denials. This second meeting of the Sanhedrin served to introduce the trial scene which followed, Jesus was "delivered over" to Pilate: the recurrence of this expression throughout the passion narrative is a reminder that all is happening "according to the definite plan and foreknowledge of God" (Acts 2:23). It is enough to name Pilate – all Christians know who he is.

Mark has firmly presented the passion of Jesus as proclamation of his kingship and the crucifixion as an enthronement. The theme appears at once in Pilate's question: "Are you the King of the Jews?" (15:2). Jesus did not reject the title out of hand but he did imply ("You say so") that he understood it differently. Pilate repeatedly calls him King of the Jews (15:9,12); indeed, in v 12 he is "the man whom you (the chief priests) call the King of the Jews." The soldiers payed homage to "the King of the Jews" (15:16-19) and the official charge against Jesus read: "The King of the Jews" (15:26). Priests and scribes mocked him as "the Messiah, the King of Israel" (15:32). If, for Mark, this is a narrative of the enthronement of Christ as king, it is such in light of Jesus' profession of 14:62 – which sealed his fate (14:63-64). Jesus' royal status is wholly paradoxical. Jesus' royal authority could never resemble the authority of earthly kings (see 10:42-45).

The priests hastened to press charges against him; Jesus preserved the silence that is a feature of the suffering Just One (see Is 53:7). Pilate's "wonder" is more than surprise; it conveys a sense of religious awe (see 5:20; John 19:8-11). Outside of the gospels we find no trace of the Passover amnesty described here (v 6); it would seem to be an inference drawn from this isolated Barabbas incident. Interestingly, Luke makes no mention of the custom. Barabbas was in prison with other rebels who had killed during a political affray. The crowd came to plead for this man, and Pilate presented them with an alternative: they might have instead "the King of the Jews." He had seen through the charges made against Jesus. Mark puts the responsibility where he believed it belonged, at the door of the priests. As in all the gospels, Pilate was convinced of Jesus' innocence, but yielded to pressure. It is he who is really on trial; John has developed this feature in masterly fashion. Pilates's strange appeal to the crowd as to what to do with this King of the Jews is very effective. It meant that the will of the crowd would be the decisive factor. The nation rejected its king and called for his death on the cross. Pilate helplessly protested Jesus' innocence – "Why, what evil has he done?" – but they clamoured for blood. Pilate yielded, "wishing to satisfy the crowd." He released a murderer and condemned an innocent man. Jesus was scourged: a severe flogging was the normal prelude to crucifixion.

Crucifixion (15:16-32)

Death by crucifixion was, and was intended to be, degrading. Even the choice of the place of Jesus' execution was a calculated insult. Archeological research has shown that Golgotha, a disused quarry, was, at that time, a refuse-dump. There was nothing of majesty about the death of Jesus, no trace of glory.

The Marcan drama reached its climax in the crucifixion scene. The evangelist had warned of Jesus' death in 3:6; from that point on, explicitly or by allusion, he continued to harp on it. In painting this scene he has drawn upon Old Testament passages portraying the figure of the suffering Just One, who suffers but is finally vindicated. Various motifs which build up the image of the Just One, taken mainly from the psalms, surface in this passage. Mark's concern is to establish that everything took place according to the scriptures, that is, according to the will of God.

It was customary for the condemned man to carry his cross beam. Mark tells us that a certain Simon of Cyrene (a town in North Africa, but perhaps Simon now lived in Palestine) was "impressed" by the soldiers to carry the beam. Alexander and Rufus were evidently known to Mark's community. Golgatha, an Aramaic name, means "a skull." The name may have been suggested by a skull-shaped hill; though the text speaks only of "place" and does not specify hill. It was presumably outside the city wall and close to a road (v 29). It was Jewish custom, based on Proverbs 31:6-7, to provide condemned criminals with drugged wine as a means of lessening their torment. Jesus, in Gethsemane, had accepted the Father's will, and accepted it wholeheartedly; he will not take the wine. And they crucified him – no more simply could the dread act be recorded. By custom, the clothes of the condemned fell to the executioners. Mark, with Ps 22:18 in mind, saw in this, too, a divine purpose.

The evangelist marks the time off in three-hourly intervals (15:25, 33, 34). For that matter, precise statements of time are a feature of the trial and passion narrative: 14:72; 15:1, 25, 33, 42; 16:1. This is to indicate that the passage of time was in accord with the will of God. Nothing at all has happened by chance or unexpectedly. The third hour is 9 a.m. It is impossible to reconcile this time reference with John 19:14 where Jesus was sentenced at 12 noon of 14 Nisan. John's purpose is to have Jesus die at the hour when the Passover lambs were slaughtered. Both evangelists are making theological statements.

The superscription (15:26) is in accordance with Roman practice; for Mark it indicates that the King is now enthroned. All the gospels agree that Jesus was crucified between two criminals. Many manuscripts of Mark carry as v 28: "And the scripture was fulfilled which says, He was reckoned with the transgressors." It is a borrowing from Lk 22:37, but it does make explicit the intent of Mark who would have seen in this disturbing fact a fulfilment of Is 13:12. Jesus who, at the arrest, had protested that he was no bandit (léstés) now is crucified between bandits. Two sets of taunts were now levelled at Jesus. The fact that there were passersby suggests crucifixion near a roadway. Their taunt was influenced by Lamentations 2:15 and Ps 22:7-8 – "They wag their heads"; "He committed his cause to the Lord; let him deliver him, let him rescue him." And they "derided", literally "blasphemed", him. They were, of course, really blaspheming God, so doing the very thing that justified Jesus' condemnation to death (14:64). Their words harked back to the Temple charge in 14:58. The irony is that precisely by not saving his life (8:35), by not coming down from the cross, Jesus was bringing the Temple to an end (15:38) and building the new temple.

The mocking invitation for Jesus to come down from the cross was echoed by the leaders of official Judaism. The presence of the chief priests and scribes at the crucifixion and their cruel railing cannot be historical. But, in Mark's storyline it is fitting that they should be the principal scoffers. They, implacable opponents of Jesus, had to be fitted in at this climactic moment. "He saved others" – a reference to Jesus' ministry of healing, regularly described as sózein, "to heal" or "to save" (e.g. 5:23, 28, 34). It is in his death that Jesus accomplished salvation and was perceived to be the Son of God. This becomes clear in the episode of 15:27-39. Here, Jesus was three times challenged – by the passersby (vv 29-30), by the religious leaders (vv 31-32a) and by those crucified with him (15:32b) – to come down from the cross and thereby save himself. Jesus would not rise to the challenge. As one who had warned the disciples, "Those who want to save their life will lose it" (8:25), and as the Son who wills what the Father wills (14:36), Jesus made no attempt to save his life. Mark is making a theological point: salvation is never of oneself, not even for Jesus. Nor is there any hope of salvation from an Elijah-figure (15:35-365).

Up to now Jesus had been "King of the Jews"; now he is "the Messiah, the King of Israel." Since Maccabean times "Jews" had become the Gentile name for the people of Israel, so King of the Jews is normal in dealing with Pilate; the priests, naturally, used "Israel" as a self-designation. Jewish tradition had anticipated that in the days of Messiah the true Israel would be established. Now Jesus is being ironically addressed as King of this echatological Israel. They are still looking for "signs" (see 8:11-12): If Jesus does come down from the cross they will "see" and believe. In Mark "seeing" is primarily associated with the "seeing" of Jesus at the *parousia* (13:26; 14:62). But there can be no "seeing" until Jesus has died and risen. Temple sayings and christological titles, prominent in 14:58 and 14:61-62, are brought together here (15:29, 32); the significance of both is being worked out on the cross. The denouement comes in 15:38-39. Meanwhile, Jesus' isolation is total: even his companions in suffering derided him (v 32b).

Mark has firmly presented the crucifixion of Jesus as an enthronement. The title appears at once in Pilate's opening question: "Are you the King of the Jews?" (15:2). Jesus accepts the designation but with the implication that he understands it differently, Pilate consistently calls him King of the Jews (vv 9,12): indeed, in v 12 he is "the one whom you call" King of the Jews. The soldiers pay homage to the "King of the Jews" (15:16-19) and the official superscription "The King of the Jews" is fixed on Jesus' cross. And priests and scribes mock him as "Christ, the King of Israel" (15:32). For Mark this is a narrative of the enthronement of Christ as king; and it can be such in light of the christological profession of 14:62. Jesus' royal status is wholly paradoxical.

Death and revelation (15:33-39)

The grim drama was being played out. Crucified at the third hour (9 a.m.), Jesus had spent three hours in agony. Now, at the sixth hour (noon), broke the hour of darkness, of momentary demonic triumph – "your hour, and the power of darkness" (Lk 2:53; see Amos 8:9-10). Jesus had begun his mission in an encounter with Satan (Mk 1:12-13) and carried on the war in his exorcisms. Now, helpless on the cross, he seemed to be crushed by these very powers. The close of that time of darkness, the ninth hour (3 p.m.), marked the hour of fulfilment. Paradoxically, it seemed to sound the nadir of Jesus' defeat. This is brought out by the twofold reference to a "loud cry." The expression *phóné megalé* occurs only four times in Mark. In 1:26 and 5:7 it is the loud cry of a demoniac, one oppressed by an evil spirit. Jesus himself now (15:34, 37) reacted with a loud cry to the intolerable pressure of evil. He suffered the absence of God: his cry of dereliction was one of total desolation: "My God, my God, why have you forsaken me?" His words are the opening of Psalm 22 – a lament. Lament is the cry of a suffering righteous person addressed to the One who can bring an end to suffering. Mark has Jesus die in total desolation, without any relieving feature at all. It would have seemed that, up to this point, Jesus' isolation could go no further: deserted by his disciples, taunted by his enemies, derided by those who hung with him, suffocating in the darkness of evil. But the worst was now: abandoned by God. His suffering was radically lonely. But his God was "my God" (v 34). Even in this, as at Gethsemane, it was "not what I want, but what you want." Here, even more than then, the sheer humanness of Jesus was manifest.

In the tragic drama of the Mark/Matthew passion narrative, Jesus has been abandoned by his disciples and mocked by all who have come to the cross. Darkness has covered the earth; there is nothing that shows God acting on Jesus' side. How appropriate that Jesus feel forsaken! His "Why?" is that of someone who has plumbed the depths of the abyss, and feels enveloped by the power of darkness. Jesus is not questioning the existence of God or the power of God to do something about what is happening; he is questioning the silence of the one whom he calls "My God." If we pay attention to the overall structure of the Mark/Matthew passion narrative, that form of addressing the deity is itself significant, for nowhere previously has Jesus ever prayed to God as "God." Mark/Matthew began the passion narrative with a prayer in which the deity was addressed by Jesus as "Father," the common form of address used by Jesus and one that captured his familial confidence that God would not make the Son go through the "hour" or drink the cup (Mk 14:35-36; Mt 26:39). Yet that filial prayer, reiterated three times, was not visibly or audibly answered; and now having endured the seemingly endless agony of the "hour" and having drunk the dregs of the cup, Jesus screams out a final prayer that is an inclusion with the first prayer. Feeling forsaken as if he were not being heard, he no longer presumes to speak intimately to the All-Powerful as "Father" but employs the address common to all human beings, "My God." (The fact that Jesus is using psalm language – a fact to which Mark does not call our attention – does not make less noticeable the unusualness of such terminology on Jesus' lips.) Mark calls our attention to this contrast between the two prayers and makes it more poignant by reporting the address in each prayer in Jesus' own tongue: "Abba" and "Eloi," thus giving the impression of words coming genuinely from Jesus' heart, as distinct from the rest of his words that have been preserved in a foreign language (Greek). As he faces the agony of death, the Marcan Jesus is portrayed as resorting to his mother tongue.[24]

The bystanders thought that Jesus called on Elijah, who was popularly believed to come to the aid of the just in tribulation. Misunderstanding hounded Jesus to the end. "Vinegar" is the Roman soldiers' *posca* – a cheap red wine. The gesture was kindly meant (v 36), but Mark, likely with Ps 69:21 in mind – "They gave me gall for food, and for my thirst they gave me vinegar to drink" – thinks of it as an addition to Jesus' misery. Again the "loud cry" is significant: it depicts Jesus' awareness of his struggle with evil. All the more so because Mark describes a sudden, violent death – "breathed his last" is not strong enough to convey his meaning (v 37). Jesus died abandoned, seemingly crushed by the forces of evil. This is perfectly in keeping with Mark's *theologia crucis*. Forthwith he can point to the victory of Jesus.

At the end of the passage 15:27-39, Mark focuses on the theme of Jesus as "the Son of God." In contrast to the mocking challenges hurled at the dying Jesus (15:29-32), there is an emphatically positive response to Jesus' death. The centurion in charge of the execution stood facing a helpless victim on a cross and watched him as he died. He declared, in awe: "Truly, this man was God's Son!" (15:39). His declaration is to be viewed in the context of the rending of the temple curtain from top to bottom (15:38). The temple had lost its significance (see 11:12-25; 13:2; 14:58). It was the end of the cult through which God had hitherto mediated forgiveness of sin and salvation. Mark's theological point is that a Jesus who had known the pang of Godforsakenness was now wholly vindicated. The temple curtain "was torn" – by God! Salvation is henceforth mediated uniquely through the shedding of his blood by the wholly faithful Son of God. Jesus had already proclaimed as much. He had done so in his words to the disciples: "For the Son of Man came not to be served but to serve, and to give his life a ransom for many" (10:45). And in his words at the last supper: "This is my blood of the covenant which is poured out for many" (14:24). The temple is gone. God's Son is henceforth the "place" of salvation. "Truly this man was God's Son." The chief priests and scribes had demanded, in mockery, "Let the Messiah, the King of Israel, come down from the cross now, so that we may see and believe" (15:32). Now, a Gentile saw and believed. His is a profession of Christian faith. It is the clincher to Mark's theological stance that the revelation of God's Son took place on the cross.

The faithful women (15:40-44)

The Twelve had fled. Yet, Jesus had not been wholly deserted – a little group of women disciples remained. Mark says of them: "They used to follow him and provided for him when he was in Galilee; and there were many other women who had come up with him to Jerusalem" (15:41). The women had "followed him" – *akolouthein* is a technical term for discipleship. Although this is the only place in the gospel where the discipleship of women is mentioned in explicit terms, we should not overlook the reference to "many other women." We must recognize that throughout the gospel, "disciple" is an inclusive term. It is because they had continued to follow him if only "at a distance" (v 40) – as women they could not be at the very place of execution – that the final message is entrusted to these women (16:1-8). They alone, of all disciples, had followed to the cross. Luke is the evangelist who gets the credit for alerting us to Jesus' solicitude for womankind. But Mark had, beforehand, made his telling contribution. The chosen male disciples had abandoned Jesus (14:50). These women disciples have stood steadfast and have not been ashamed of Jesus. They are those of whom the Son of Man will not be ashamed (8:38).

The burial (15:42-47)

The story of Jesus' burial was important because it established that Jesus had really died and because it assured that the women had seen where the body had been placed. This was crucial in view of the manner of the burial. Mark sticks to his three-hour scheme even though the "evening" (6 p.m.) would mean that the sabbath had begun. The "day of preparation" (v 42) – here is where we learn that Jesus died on a Friday. The Twelve had fled at the arrest of Jesus (14:50). It was left to another to bury him. Joseph of Arimathea, a Sanhedrin member, was concerned to fulfil the law – here, that the body of one hanged should not be left overnight on the tree (Dt 21:23).

Joseph was duly granted the corpse of Jesus (Mk 15:42-46). It would be a hasty, dishonourable burial of one executed on a charge of blasphemy. The body was not anointed. It was simply wrapped in a linen shroud and placed in a niche of that disused quarry. A far cry, indeed, from the royal burial of the fourth gospel (Jn 19:38-42). We need to be sensitive to the theological concerns of the evangelists. The only witnesses of the burial were women, a preparation for the final passage of the gospel (16:1-8).

CONCLUSION

In some respects the painful Gethsemane episode (Mk 14:32-42, parr.) is the most comforting in the gospels. There we see Jesus at his most human. Hitherto, he had gone resolutely to meet his fate. Now that the dreadful moment is upon him, "he began to be distressed and agitated" (14:33) – it is difficult to convey adequately the force of Mark's Greek: Jesus was shattered.

Triumph of failure

It had been dawning on Jesus what it was the Father seemed to be asking of him. He needed to be assured that what God seemed to be asking he really did ask: "Abba, Father, for you all things are possible; remove this cup from me; yet not what I want but what you want" (14:36). This is the first and only time, in Mark's gospel, that Jesus is said to have spoken the Aramaic "Abba" – the familiar title seems wrenched from him at this awful moment. He prayed, explicitly, that the cup be taken from him. He did not contemplate suffering and death with stoical calm. He was appalled at the prospect; he knew fear. He was brave as he rose above his dread to embrace what it was the Father asked. But he must know if the path that opened before him was indeed the way his God would have him walk. He found assurance in prayer (14:35-36, 39). His prayer did not go unanswered. As the epistle to the Hebrews puts it: "he was heard because of his reverent submission" (Heb 5:7). In traditional biblical imagery, Luke has dramatized the heavenly response: "Then an angel from heaven appeared to him and gave him strength" (Lk 22:43). Jesus was assured that it was indeed the Father's will that he tread the lonely way of total rejection. Not the Father's will as part of some cold, inflexible design. The Father was prepared to make a supreme sacrifice: "Surely, they will respect my Son!" (Mk 12:6). Jesus had understood that just here lay the victory over evil. For evil is finally helpless before a love that will never cry: Enough!

Failure?

The truth of the matter is that his death marked Jesus as historically a failure. Jesus was executed on the order of a Roman provincial official: an alleged trouble-maker in that bothersome province of Judea had been dealt with. The incident did not raise a ripple in imperial affairs. Yet history has shown that this execution was an event of historic proportions. Its ripples flow stronger than ever two thousand years later.

Let us be clear about it. The Romans and the Jewish Sanhedrin had effectively closed the "Jesus case". The aims and message of Jesus, and his life itself, had ended in death. His prophetic voice had been muzzled. This is failure. The question is: Why had Jesus been silenced? It was because he, unflinchingly, had lived and preached God's love for humankind. That is why he had table fellowship with sinners, why he sought to free women and men from the tyranny of religion, why he, at every hand's turn, bore witness to the true God. He might, in face of the threatening opposition, have packed it in and gone home to Nazareth. That would have been real failure. But he would not be turned from witnessing to God's love. They might take his life, but to his last breath he would witness. What Jesus tells us is that failure is not the last word. That is, as God views failure.

From God's point of view, in the fate of Jesus there could be no question of failure. This is what John brings out, dramatically, in his gospel. He undoubtedly knew the tradition behind the synoptic gospels but he chose to turn their tragedy into triumph. What is important for us in his presentation is that he understood what the others imply: failure is not the last word. But what Mark has done is of equal importance: he has shown that a sense of failure, even for Jesus, is a grievous human experience.

Theology of the cross

It is not enough to declare that Mark is a *theologia crucis*; one must, to some extent, spell out what it means. Here is an attempt to do just that. God is revealed with unwonted clarity in one human life and in one episode of human history. If Jesus is image of the invisible God (see Col 1:15), the cross is revelation of true God and true humankind. On the cross Jesus shows what it is to be human. God's Son dramatically demonstrates the radical powerlessness of the human being. He shows us that we are truly human when we accept our humanness, when we face up to the fact that we are not masters of our fate. The cross offers the authentic definition of humanness: God's definition. There, he starkly and firmly reminds us of who and what we are.

On the cross God defined the human being as creature – not to crush or humiliate, but that he might be, as Creator, wholly with his creature. On its own, humankind has indeed reason to fear. With God, in total dependence on God, there is no place for fear. The resurrection of Jesus makes that clear. For the resurrection is God's endorsement of the definition of humankind established on the cross. And it is God's endorsement of the definition of God established there. It is here he defined himself over against all human caricatures of him. God, in the cross, is a radical challenge to our hubris, our pride. He is the God who has entered, wholly, into rejection and humiliation and suffering. He is the God present in human life where to human eyes he is absent. He is the God of humankind. He is God *for us*.

Conclusion

"Who, then, is this?" – a question that has stood over the whole of this study. I have sought to discern, and present, Mark's answer to the question. I am quite sure that Mark's own answer is true and profound. I would hope that my discernment and presentation have been fair to Mark. If the reader now has a better appreciation of his gospel and is pointed to a closer reading of it, my purpose has been achieved. One cannot come to Mark without acquiring a clearer understanding of Jesus and a keener awareness of the challenge of discipleship.

The object of Christian faith is a living person, Jesus of Nazareth.He lived in the first century AD. He died – but lives forever, glorified, in the Father's presence. We have access to our living Lord through faith. The historical Jesus is not the object of our faith. He ought to be an integral part of our christology. Dialogue with the historical Jesus guards our theology from degenerating into ideology.

Jesus of Nazareth was a prophet with a burning desire for the renewal of his people as God's holy elect. His challenge and his invitation were to all. He proclaimed the kingdom – the Rule of God. The God of Jesus is a God with supreme concern for people. His rule, his lordship, envisaged an ideal relationship between God and humankind. Jesus lived and died for the establishment of that rule. He ached for men and women to discover the love of God for humankind and give substance to the wonder of the discovery in loving concern for one another.

Jesus preached the kingdom: he preached that God is the ultimate meaning of this world. The Rule of God does not signify something "spiritual," outside of this world; it is not "pie in the sky." Jesus was supremely concerned with our real world. He spoke so vaguely of the future that the first Christians could expect that the end would come in their day (see Mk 9:1; 13:20). When he preached the kingdom of God he envisaged a revolution in the existing order. He made two fundamental demands: he asked for personal conversion and he postulated a restructuring of the human world. Conversion (*metanoia*) meant changing one's mode of thinking and acting to suit God's purpose for humankind. It would be a new manner of existing before God.

But conversion also meant a turning from the established order. Jesus made the point, so clearly grasped and effectively developed by Paul, that it is not law that saves – not even the Law – it is love. Jesus' outlook and conduct were marked by freedom. His understanding of freedom is again faithfully reflected by Paul: freedom to serve. Jesus did not make life easier. His disconcerting word was that love knows no limits. He proclaimed not law but good news. The gospel is good news for one who can grasp its spirit and react positively to it. His good news embraced basic equality: all men and women, as children of the Father, are brothers and sisters. Good news so understood is a radical challenge to all social and ecclesiastical systems based on power.

The prophet Jesus was in the line, too, of the sages of Israel. He taught the people. As teacher, no less than as prophet, he sought disciples. He called, and his call was a powerful summons. Discipleship meant wholehearted commitment – it was no soft option. His principle was that religion was meant to enable men and women to attain authentic humanness; it was not meant to enslave them. He took a firm stand against legalism. In light of God's preferential option for the poor, he warned of the threat of riches. Jesus was no respecter of persons. His declaration, "It is easier for a camel to go through the eye of a needle than for someone who is rich to enter the kingdom of God" (10:25) would not be welcome in certain quarters. The gist of his teaching is found in his startling assertion that the essence of authority is service. If this were grasped and lived, much else would fall together. Until it is grasped and lived, authority in the church will continue to forfeit respect.

Jesus was worker of miracles. In the main his activity was in the area of healing and covered a range of afflictions. He cured illness only in response to faith. Surely his deepest healing was at another level. His practice of table fellowship with sinners must have touched hearts. Mark perceptively observed that his "healing" had overtones of "saving" *(sózein)*. And his opening of the eyes of the blind was an opening to more than the light of our world. A distinctive mode of healing was evidenced in the exorcisms. Here Jesus struck at the heart of evil. He shared the apocalyptic worldview of his day. Good and evil were pitted in definitive struggle. His victories over evil were a presage of the undoubted ultimate victory of good. They were, already, earnest of the inbreak of the Rule of God – the kingdom.

At a turning-point in his gospel, credibly reflecting a turning-point in the ministry of Jesus, Mark has Jesus ask his disciples: "Who do you say that I am?" (Mk 8:29). Peter gave his straightforward reply: "You are the Christ (Messiah)," and then went on to demonstrate that he had a wholly mistaken notion of that messiahship as he rejected Jesus' words on suffering and death (8:29-32). The question to the disciples is addressed to every Christian. It is salutary to recall that the first answer, while seemingly correct, was in reality wide of the mark. Peter was not the first disciple, nor the last, whose understanding of Jesus does not match the titles so readily bestowed. Here is the first of the three "predictions of the passion" (8:31; 9:31; 10:33-34), unquestionably, as they stand, *vaticinia ex eventu*. It is not, however, surprising that, towards the end, Jesus should have foreseen the likelihood, the probability indeed, of violent death. Nevertheless, at Gethsemane, he was faced with a painful decision. He had preached the Rule of God, had striven to make it a reality. Now it must seem to him that his mission faced the ultimate frustration: his prophetic voice will be stilled in death.

"God was in Christ, reconciling the world to himself" (2 Cor 5:19). As Christians, we see our God in Jesus of Nazareth. If we are to let God be God, we must let Jesus be Jesus. Christology – theological understanding of Jesus Christ – cannot be unveiling of mystery. We must let the mystery abide. And the mystery is the person Jesus of Nazareth. To diminish his human reality is to screen from sight the God who would shine through him. Christology has tended to do just that. We need to acknowledge a vulnerable Jesus if we are to meet our vulnerable God.[25] The mystery of Jesus is that in him God communicates himself in a full and unrestricted manner. Jesus' divinity is not, as sometimes presented, some kind of second substance in him. His divinity consists in the fact that, as the perfect counterpart of God, he is the manifestation and presence of God in our world. Any misperception that "Jesus is human, but...," and it is all too common, is, effectively, refusal of the God who revealed himself in Jesus. When the human Jesus is not acknowledged, our understanding of God suffers and our Christianity suffers. This is not to say that the full reality of Jesus may be adequately summed up under the rubric "human being" – there is something other, something much more. But his human wholeness must be acknowledged.

The career of Jesus did not end on the cross. The resurrection is God's endorsement of the definition of both God and humankind made on the cross. Just as the death of Jesus cannot be detached from the life lived before it, his resurrection cannot be detached from his career and death. Because he was raised from the dead, Jesus holds decisive significance for us. Because of the fact of his resurrection we know that meaningless death – and, often, meaningless life – has meaning. Jesus died with the cry on his lips, "My God, my God, why have you forsaken me?" The sequel was to show that God had not forsaken Jesus. We have the assurance that he will never abandon us. While, unlike his immediate disciples, we do not follow the steps of Jesus from Galilee to Jerusalem, we do join his human pilgrimage from birth to death. His word of promise is that we shall follow him beyond death to share his rest (see Heb 12:2). We shall know fully our Abba at last and become wholly his children.

Notes

1. Harrington, Wilfrid J., O.P., *Revelation. Sacra Pagina 16*. A Michael Glazier Book. (Collegeville, MN: The Liturgical Press, 1993); Wilfrid Harrington, O.P., *Revelation. Proclaiming a Vision of Hope* (San Jose: Resource Publications, 1994).

2. "Theologal life (the intense dialogue between human beings and God) is concentrated in a unique way in Christ, because in him there is a fullness of relations between Father and Son. Our theologal life is a participation in the life of Christ, in his filial relationship with God. We participate in the relationship between Father and Son. Only Jesus is interpersonal relationship; we merely take part. Here is the uniqueness of Jesus Christ." Edward Schillebeeckx, *I Am a Happy Theologian*. Conversations with Francesco Stragazzi (London: SCM 1994), 58.

3. See D. Rhoads and D. Michie, *Mark as Story* (Philadelphia: Fortress, 1982).

4. Olsen, R. A., "Mark 16:1-8," *Interpretation* (1993), 409.

5. Schneiders, Sandra M., *The Revelatory Text. Interpreting the New Testament as Sacred Scripture* (San Francisco: Harper, 1991), 107-108.

6. Meier, John P., *A Marginal Jew*. Vol. I. Rethinking the Historical Jesus. (New York: Doubleday, 1991).

7. Murphy-O'Connor, Jerome, "John the Baptist and Jesus: History and Hypotheses," *New Testament Studies 36* (1990), 359-374.

8. Meier, John P., *A Marginal Jew*. Vol. 2. Mentor, Message, and Miracles. (New York: Doubleday. 1994), 414. See pp. 237-506.

9. Schillebeeckx, Edward, (op. cit., p.54) links the reign or rule of God with the fact that human beings are in the image of God.

"Human beings are God's image where and when they do justice, respect the integrity of creation, practise solidarity. It can be said that where God reigns, human beings have the right to be human. In their humanity men and women manifest the reign of God in history. And it is men and women who mediate the presence of the kingdom of God. Clearly the kingdom of God is God, the gratuitousness of God mediated through human beings."

10. Op. cit., 308-309.

11. Drury, John, *The Parables in The Gospels*. History and Allegory. (London: SPCK, 1985).

12. Wright, Addison G., "The Widow's Mite: Praise or Lament? A Matter of Context," CBQ 44 (1982), 256-262.

13. Schillebeeckx, Edward, op. cit, 59.

"A religion which damages and destroys human beings and human dignity is a religion which denies itself. A religion which humiliates human beings is, by definition, a mistaken way of believing in God and at least a religion which has lost any sense of its own interpretation and contact with its authentic roots."

14. Op. cit., 512.

15. The criterion of multiple attestation focuses on sayings or deeds of Jesus present in more than one literary source (e.g. Mark, Paul, John). The criterion of coherence maintains that sayings or deeds of Jesus which fit well with data established by other criteria are presumably historical.

16. Op. cit., 787.

17. Op. cit., 406-407.

18. Brown, R. E., *The Death of the Messiah*, 2 vols. (New York: Doubleday, 1994.

19. Meier, J.P., op. cit., 450.

20. Op. cit., 966.

21. Brown, R. E. op. cit., 513,

22. Kingsbury, J. D., *The Christology of Mark's Gospel* (Philadelphia: Fortress, 1983), 66.

23. Brown, R. E., op. cit., 625.

24. Brown, R. E., op. cit., 1046.

25. Harrington, W., *The Tears of God*, (Collegeville: Liturgical Press, 1992).

For Reference and Further Study

Mark

Paul J. Achtemeir, *Mark* . (Philadelphia: Fortress, 1975).

John R. Donahue, *The Gospel of Mark.* (Collegeville, MN: The Liturgical Press, 2002).

Ernest Best, *Mark. The Gospel as Story.* (Edinburgh: T.& T. Clark, 1983).

Daniel J. Harrington, "The Gospel According to Mark," *The New Jerome Biblical Commentary*, R. E. Brown, J. A. Fitzmyer, R. E. Brown, eds. (Englewood Cliffs, N. J.: Prentice Hall, 1989), 596-629.

Wilfrid J. Harrington, *Mark.* (Revised) (Wilmington, DE: M. Glazier, 1985)

Wilfrid J. Harrington, *The Jesus Story.* A Michael Glazier Book (Collegevile, MN: Liturgical Press, 1991).

Martin Hengel, *Studies in the Gospel of Mark.* (Philadelphia: Fortress, 1985).

Jack D. Kingsbury, *The Christology of Mark's Gospel* (Philadelphia: Fortress, 1983).

Jack D. Kingsbury, *Conflict in Mark: Jesus, Authorities, Disciples,* (Minneapolis: Fortress, 1989).

Denis E. Nineham, *Saint Mark* (Baltimore: Penguin Books, 1963).

D. Rhoads & D. Michie, *Mark as Story* (Philadelphia: Fortress,1982).

Edward Schweizer, *The Good News According to Mark.* (Richmond, VA: John Knox Press, 1970).

Donald Senior, *The Passion of Jesus in the Gospel of Mark* (Wilmington, DE: M. Glazier, 1984).

Augustine Stock, *The Method and Message of Mark*. (Wilmington, DE: M. Glazier, 1985).

Bonnie Bowman Thurston, *Preaching Mark*. (Minneapolis: Fortress Press, 2002).

Lamar Williamson, *Mark* [Interpretation]. (Louisville: John Knox, 1983).

Interpretation 47 (1993), No. 4. The Gospel of Mark.

General

Graham Stanton, *The Gospels and Jesus*. [2nd ed.] (Oxford: OUP, 2002).

Raymond E. Brown, *The Death of the Messiah*. Two vols. (New York: Doubleday, 1994)

John Drury, *The Parables in the Gospels* (New York: Crossroad, 1985).

John P. Meier, *A Marginal Jew*. Vol. 1. *Rethinking the Historical Jesus*; Vol. 2. *Mentor, Message, and Miracles*, (New York: Doubleday, 1991, 1994).

Edward Schillebeeckx, *Jesus: An Experiment in Christology*. (New York: Crossroad, 1981).

Sandra M. Schneiders, *The Revelatory Text. Interpreting the New Testament as Sacred Scripture* (San Francisco: Harper, 1991).

Index to Marcan Passages

1:1	121	8:34–38	118
1:11	121	9:2–8	109f
1:14–15	32	9:14–29	92
1:16–20	35	9:30–32	36, 116
1:22–28	88f	9:38–40	94
1:29–31	75	10:2–12	62f
1:40–45	76f, 84	10:17–31	65f
2:1–3:6	42f	10:23–27	67
2:1–12	114	10:33–34	36, 107, 116
2:17	99	10:35–45	58f
2:19–20	101	10:45	117
2:23–26	115	10:46–52	83f
3:1–6	77f	11:1–11	38, 106, 121
3:13–19	35	11:15–18	39f
3:20–35	43f	12:1–12	44f
4:1–34	51f	12:13–17	64f
4:1-9	52f	12:18–27	69f
4:10–12	51f	12:38-44	67f
4:14–20	52f	12:41-44	68f
4:26–29	54	13:24–27	118f
4:30–32	55	13:33–37	55
5:1–20	89ff	13:38–44	67f
5:21–43	78ff	14:1–25	37f, 40
6:1–6	41f	14:17–21	117
6:35–44	102f	14:27–28	38, 111
7:1–22	60f	14:61	119
7:24–30	91f	14:66–72	129f
7:31–37	81	15:1–15	130f
8:1–9	102f	15:6–32	113
8:14–21	105f	15:16–32	131f
8:22–26	81ff	15:33–39	134f
8:29–30	97	15:40–44	137
8:31	36	15:42–47	138, 29
8:32–33	107f	16:1–8	17f
8:34–9:1	56f		